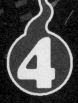

YOKAI GIRLS

KIYOMIZU

Yanagimori Shrine

D0885447

Please no littering

Chiyo

HI GH

Funatsu Kazuki

4

The Cast of Monster Girls!

NISHIZURU NANAO

Yatsuki's sister. She's been stuck as a spirit for the past six years, unable to return to her comatose body.

NISHIZURU YATSUKI

Works part-time in Akihabara. Can see ghosts, and got himself mixed up with a bunch of yokai.

YOU'RE GETTING CARRIED AWAY...

KAPPERVERT-SAN!!

AYATSUKI ROKKA

A pretty girl whom Yatsuki once helped out. She seems quite taken with him since then. She's actually a yokai: a rokurokubi.

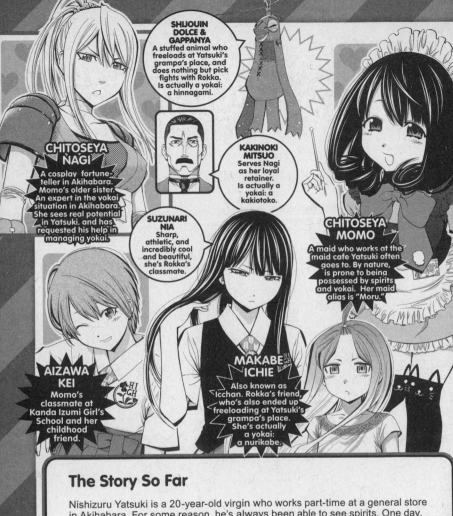

SHIJOUIN DOLCE & GAPPANYA
A stuffed animal who freeloads at Yatsuki's grampa's place, and does nothing but pick fights with Rokka. Is actually a yokai: a hinnagami.

CHITOSEYA NAGI
A cosplay fortune-teller in Akihabara. Momo's older sister. An expert in the yokai situation in Akihabara. She sees real potential in Yatsuki, and has requested his help in managing yokai.

KAKINOKI MITSUO
Serves Nagi as her loyal retainer. Is actually a yokai: a kakiotoko.

SUZUNARI NIA
Sharp, athletic, and incredibly cool and beautiful, she's Rokka's classmate.

CHITOSEYA MOMO
A maid who works at the maid cafe Yatsuki often goes to. By nature, is prone to being possessed by spirits and yokai. Her maid alias is "Moru."

AIZAWA KEI
Momo's classmate at Kanda Izumi Girl's School and her childhood friend.

MAKABE ICHIE
Also known as Icchan. Rokka's friend, who's also ended up freeloading at Yatsuki's grampa's place. She's actually a yokai: a nurikabe.

The Story So Far

Nishizuru Yatsuki is a 20-year-old virgin who works part-time at a general store in Akihabara. For some reason, he's always been able to see spirits. One day, he meets the beautiful Rokka. Happenstance brings them very close very fast... or it would have, but Rokka turns out to be a yokai--a rokurokubi!

Since then, a ton of yokai-related incidents have occurred in Yatsuki's life! Yatsuki has started doing "yokai management" under Nagi's tutelage in order to save his little sister, Nanao, who has been stuck as a spirit for six years now.

Meanwhile, Rokka has started attending the same school as Momo. When they rescued Kei from possession by a kappa, Momo inevitably finds out that Rokka is a yokai. The two remain friends despite this, though. Now, Rokka has become curious about their mysterious classmate, Suzunari Nia...

YOKAI GIRLS

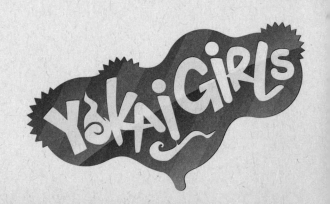

PLEASE!!
30 Meow-Meow! ♪
TELL MORU-CHAN THAT I'M JUST HUMAN!!
SHE TOTALLY THINKS THAT I'M A YOKAI!!
HUUUH? I DUNNO... YOU HAVEN'T BEEN ALL THAT NICE TO ME LATELY, JUNKER-SAN.
WIGGLE
WIGGLE
WIGGLE
JUST THE OTHER DAY, YOU SUDDENLY RIPPED MY PANTIES OFF, YEP.
And you smacked my butt!
I DIDN'T RIP YOUR PANTIES OFF!
And that was because of a yokai!
STILL, YOU NORMALLY WOULDN'T DO THAT TO A GIRL OUT OF THE BLUE, WOULD YOU?
URK!
F-FINE!
I'LL TAKE YOU TO A SPECIAL CURRY SHOP!
As an apology!
!
BEAM
REALLY?!
B-BUT JUST ONE BOWL!
Got it?!
......
Jeez, talk about stingy.

30
Meow-Meow!
♪
Yield
CONSIDERATION FOR PEOPLE, FOR CARS, FOR THIS CITY
MANSEIBASHI POLICE STATION
CHIYODA DISTRICT
SOUP CURRY KAMUÍ
Open
SOUP CURRY
VILEZON VANGUARD

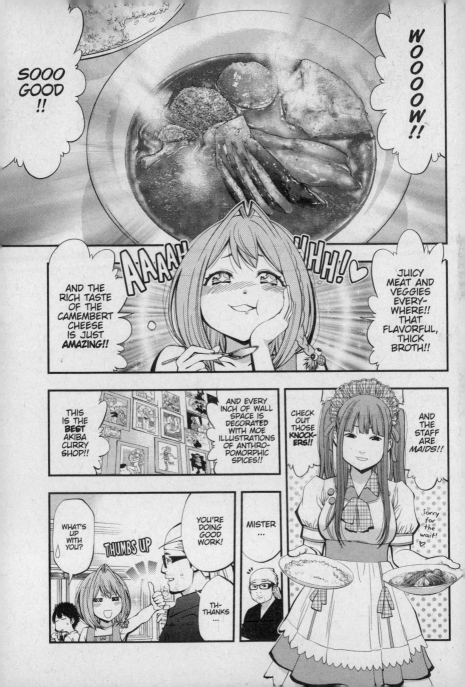

SOOO GOOD!!

WOOOOW!!

AAAAHHHH! ♥

AND THE RICH TASTE OF THE CAMEMBERT CHEESE IS JUST **AMAZING!!**

JUICY MEAT AND VEGGIES EVERY-WHERE!! THAT FLAVORFUL, THICK BROTH!!

THIS IS THE **BEST** AKIBA CURRY SHOP!!

AND EVERY INCH OF WALL SPACE IS DECORATED WITH MOE ILLUSTRATIONS OF ANTHRO-POMORPHIC SPICES!!

CHECK OUT THOSE KNOCK-ERS!!

AND THE STAFF ARE **MAIDS!!**

Sorry for the wait!

WHAT'S UP WITH YOU?

YOU'RE DOING GOOD WORK!

THUMBS UP

MISTER...

TH-THANKS...

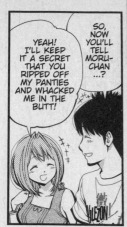

YEAH! I'LL KEEP IT A SECRET THAT YOU RIPPED OFF MY PANTIES AND WHACKED ME IN THE BUTT!

SO, NOW YOU'LL TELL MORU-CHAN...?

GLAD YOU LIKED IT!

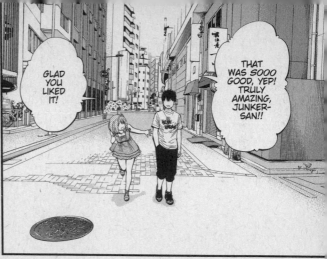

THAT WAS SOOO GOOD, YEP! TRULY AMAZING, JUNKER-SAN!!

HEY! Y-YOU... THAT'S NOT FAIR!!

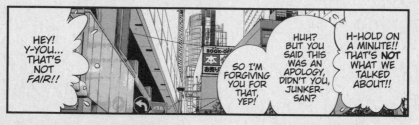

SO I'M FORGIVING YOU FOR THAT, YEP!

HUH? BUT YOU SAID THIS WAS AN APOLOGY, DIDN'T YOU, JUNKER-SAN?

H-HOLD ON A MINUTE!! THAT'S **NOT** WHAT WE TALKED ABOUT!!

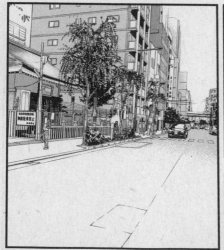

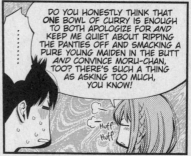

DO YOU HONESTLY THINK THAT ONE BOWL OF CURRY IS ENOUGH TO BOTH APOLOGIZE FOR AND KEEP ME QUIET ABOUT RIPPING THE PANTIES OFF AND SMACKING A PURE YOUNG MAIDEN IN THE BUTT AND CONVINCE MORU-CHAN, TOO? THERE'S SUCH A THING AS ASKING TOO MUCH, YOU KNOW!

Huff Huff

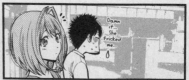

Damn it... she tricked me.

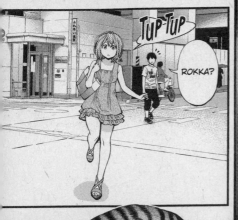

TUP·TUP

ROKKA?

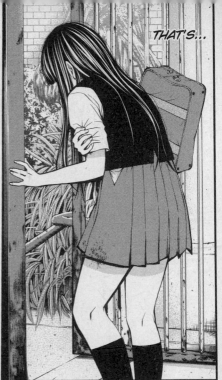

THAT'S...

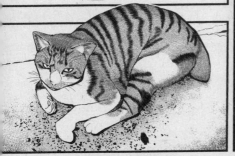

SUCH A BIG PUSSY CAT!

WHAT IS THIS? YOU'RE SO CUTE! ♡

PET PET PET

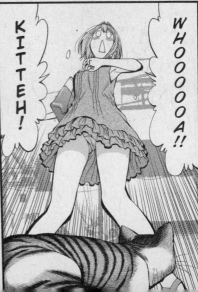

KITTEH!

WHOOOOOA!!

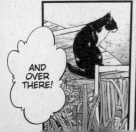

AND OVER THERE!

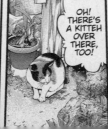

OH! THERE'S A KITTEH OVER THERE, TOO!

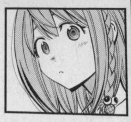

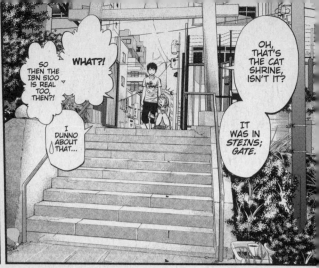

SO THEN THE IBN 5100 IS REAL TOO, THEN?!

WHAT?!

OH, THAT'S THE CAT SHRINE, ISN'T IT?

I DUNNO ABOUT THAT...

IT WAS IN STEINS;GATE.

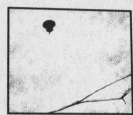

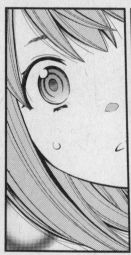

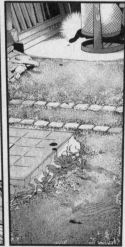

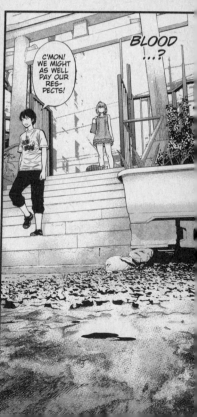

C'MON! WE MIGHT AS WELL PAY OUR RES-PECTS!

BLOOD ...?

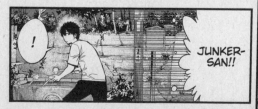

!

JUNKER-SAN!!

THIS ONE...

IS HURT!!

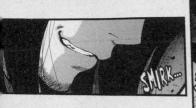

SMIRK... *ZU*

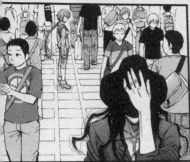

LOOKS LIKE...

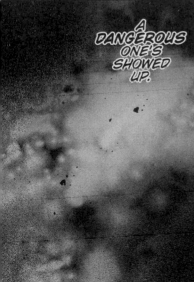

A DANGEROUS ONE'S SHOWED UP.

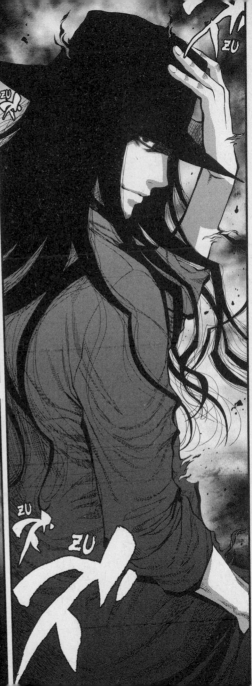

ZU

ZU

ZU

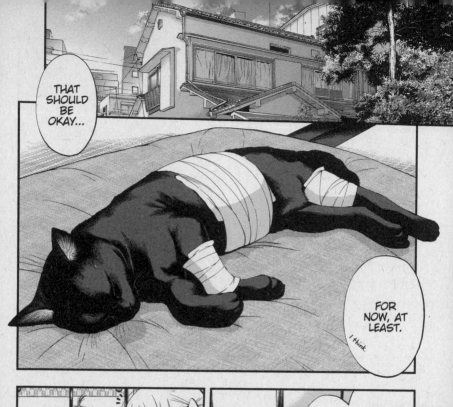

THAT SHOULD BE OKAY...

FOR NOW, AT LEAST.

I think.

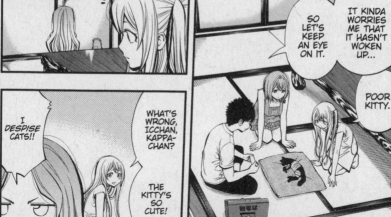

SO LET'S KEEP AN EYE ON IT.

IT KINDA WORRIES ME THAT IT HASN'T WOKEN UP...

POOR KITTY.

I DESPISE CATS!!

WHAT'S WRONG, ICCHAN, KAPPA-CHAN?

THE KITTY'S SO CUTE!

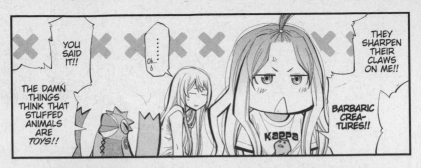

YOU SAID IT!!

THE DAMN THINGS THINK THAT STUFFED ANIMALS ARE TOYS!!

......

Oh...

THEY SHARPEN THEIR CLAWS ON ME!!

BARBARIC CREATURES!!

Kappa

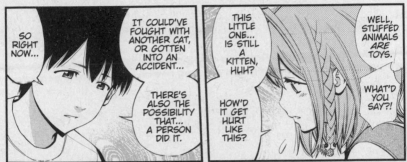

SO RIGHT NOW...

IT COULD'VE FOUGHT WITH ANOTHER CAT, OR GOTTEN INTO AN ACCIDENT...

THERE'S ALSO THE POSSIBILITY THAT... A PERSON DID IT.

THIS LITTLE ONE... IS STILL A KITTEN, HUH?

HOW'D IT GET HURT LIKE THIS?

WELL, STUFFED ANIMALS ARE TOYS.

WHAT'D YOU SAY?!

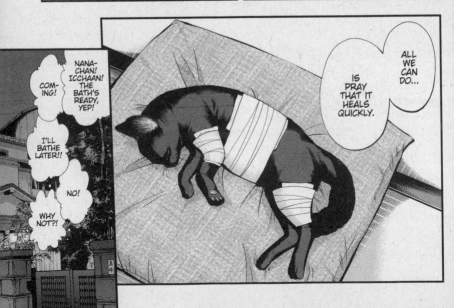

ALL WE CAN DO...

IS PRAY THAT IT HEALS QUICKLY.

NANA-CHAN! ICCHAAN! THE BATH'S READY, YEP!

COMING!

I'LL BATHE LATER!!

NO!

WHY NOT?!

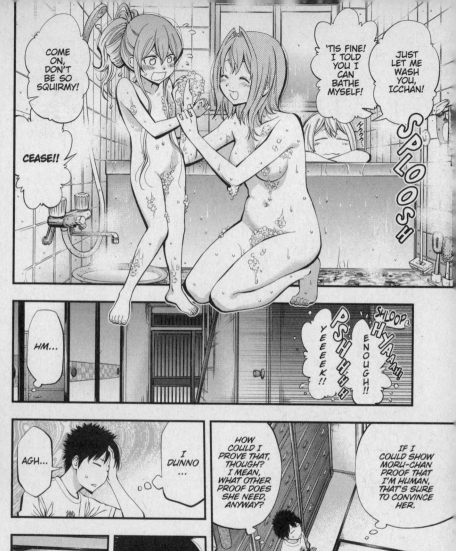

COME ON, DON'T BE SO SQUIRMY!

CEASE!!

'TIS FINE! I TOLD YOU I CAN BATHE MYSELF!

JUST LET ME WASH YOU, ICCHAN!

SPLOOSH

HM...

YEEEEK!!

PSHHHH

ENOUGH!!

HYAAH!

SHLOOP

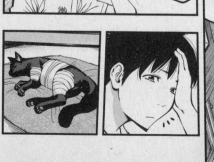

AGH...

I DUNNO...

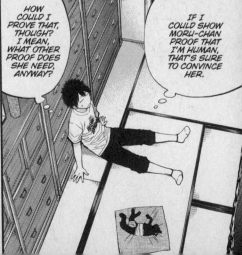

HOW COULD I PROVE THAT, THOUGH? I MEAN, WHAT OTHER PROOF DOES SHE NEED, ANYWAY?

IF I COULD SHOW MORI-CHAN PROOF THAT I'M HUMAN, THAT'S SURE TO CONVINCE HER.

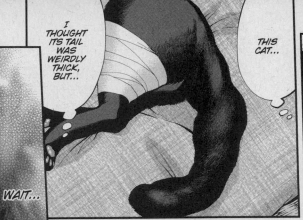

I THOUGHT ITS TAIL WAS WEIRDLY THICK, BUT...

WAIT...

THIS CAT...

HUH?

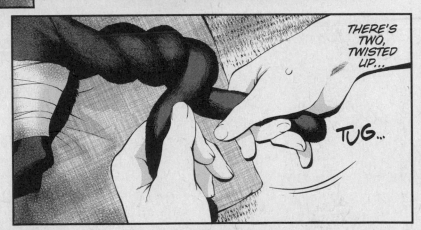

THERE'S TWO, TWISTED UP...

TUG...

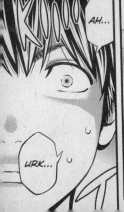

KOOOO

AH...

URK...

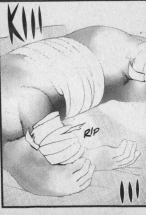

KIII

RIP

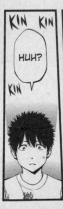

KIN KIN

HUH?

KIN

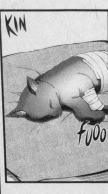

KIN

FUOO

PA—POOOF

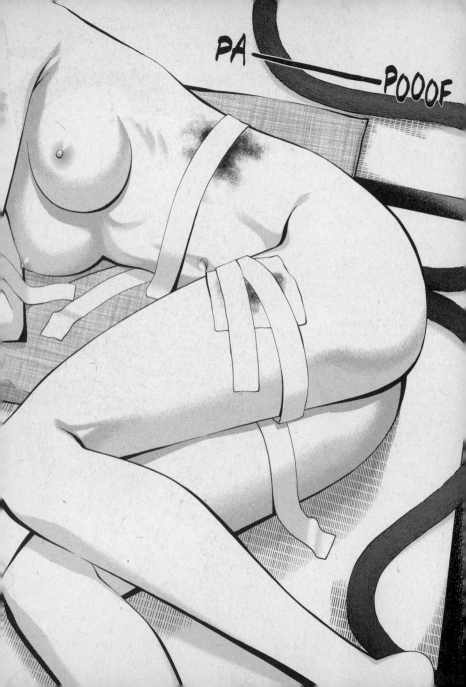

WHAAAAAAAAAAH?!!
!
LURCH'
HUH ?!
WHO THE HELL ARE...
VILEZON

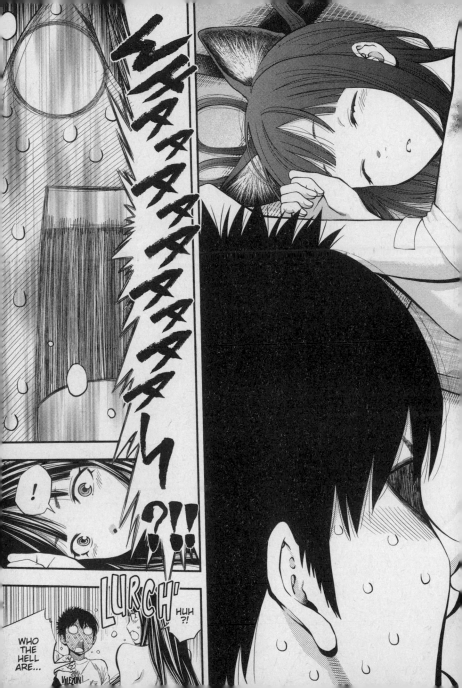

YOU...?
WH-WH-WH-WHAT THE MEOW DID YOU DO TO ME?!
MRROOOOOW
TELL ME MEOW!
NO... I DIDN'T--!
FLINCH
I DIDN'T DO ANY-MEOW TO YOU!!
TMP TMP TMP
WHAT'S GOING ON?!
JUNKER-SAN?!
HOW CAN YOU BRING WOMEN IN HERE WHILE WE'RE IN THE BATH?!
WAAAUGH!!!
VILE! 'TIS TRULY UNCOUTH!
ONIICHAN... NANAO DOESN'T THINK THAT SORT OF THING IS OKAY.
Y-Y-Y-YOU'VE GOT THE WRONG IDEA!!!

THIS IS, UM...
WAIT... HUH?!
!
YOU'RE ...
THE GIRL WITH THE PEEP--
MEOW MEOW!!
MEOW ?!!
MEOW... MYA-MEOW...
ME-YEAH !!
NO...
WAY.
WOBBLE...
I HAD NO IDEA THAT YOU AND NIA-SAN HAD THAT KIND OF RELATION-SHIP.
SLUMP...
SOB SOB SOB SOB SOB
WHAT THE MEOW ARE YOU GETTING AT?!
IT'S NOT LIKE THAT!!
HUH?
WAIT, WHERE DID THE KITTEN GO?
?
......
This girl...
LISTEN ...
UM...
YOU SEE...

POINT
HUH?
'TIS HER, YES?
YOU'RE... A BAKE-NEKO.
OR... NO...
A NEKOMATA, RIGHT?
MYA-MEOOOW...
....

Extra: Moru making cosplay outfits

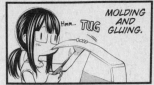

MOLDING AND GLUING.

Hmm... TUG

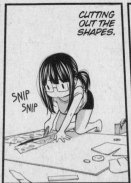

CUTTING OUT THE SHAPES.

SNIP SNIP

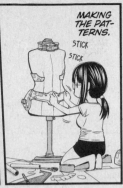

MAKING THE PATTERNS.

STICK STICK

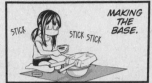

MAKING THE BASE.

STICK STICK STICK

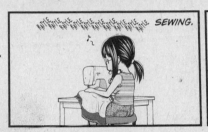

SEWING.

RATTLE RATTLE RATTLE RATTLE RATTLE RATTLE RATTLE RATTLE RATTLE RATTLE RATTLE

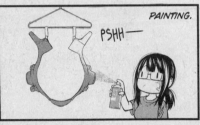

PAINTING.

PSHH—

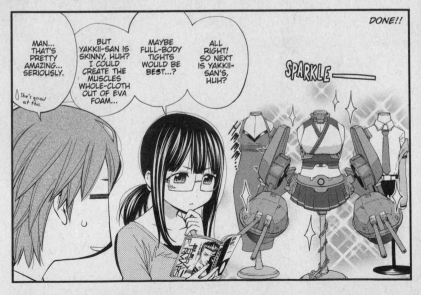

DONE!!

MAN... THAT'S PRETTY AMAZING... SERIOUSLY.

She's good at this.

BUT YAKKII-SAN IS SKINNY, HUH? I COULD CREATE THE MUSCLES WHOLE-CLOTH OUT OF EVA FOAM...

MAYBE FULL-BODY TIGHTS WOULD BE BEST...?

ALL RIGHT! SO NEXT IS YAKKII-SAN'S, HUH?

SPARKLE —————

31
Friends!
♪

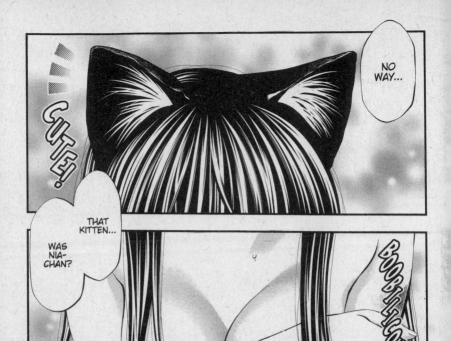

NO
WAY...

CUTE!

THAT
KITTEN...

WAS
NIA-
CHAN?

BOOBILICIOUS!

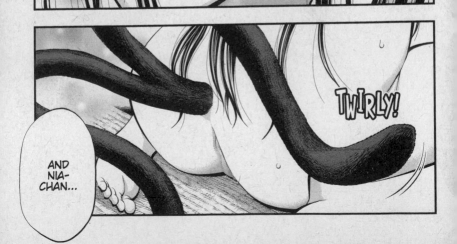

TWIRLY!

AND
NIA-
CHAN...

IS A NEKOMATA?!
MYA-MEOOOW!
NEKO-MATA:
THE "NEKOMATA," A CAT YOKAI, HAS A TAIL THAT SPLITS INTO TWO. IT IS SAID THAT AN ELDERLY CAT WILL EVENTU-ALLY BECOME A NEKOMATA. THE CREATURE EXHIBITS A VARIETY OF DAN-GEROUS BEHAVIORS AND IS EVEN SAID TO DEVOUR PEOPLE.
FOR THAT REASON, A SUPERSTITIOUS BELIEF HAS BEEN PASSED DOWN THROUGH GENERATIONS SAYING THAT EL-DERLY CATS SHOULDN'T BE KEPT AS PETS. THERE IS ALSO A FOLK BELIEF FROM VARIOUS REGIONS IN JAPAN STATING THAT WHEN AN ELDERLY CAT LEAVES ITS HOME, IT GOES INTO THE MOUNTAINS TO BECOME A NEKOMATA. ANOTHER THEORY SAYS THAT WHEN A CAT LICKS HUMAN BLOOD, IT TURNS INTO A NEKOMATA.
HEY, HOLD ON A MINUTE! WHY'D YOU LOOK AT MY CHEST JUST NOW?!
Ears and tails aside!
EH HEH HEH! ♡
I got a nice eyeful! ♡

OH!

HM?

YOU'VE NOTICED, HAVEN'T YOU?

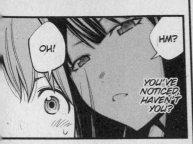

YOU'RE ONLY REALIZING THAT NOW?!

NO WAAAY!!

YOU'RE A YOKAI, NIA-CHAN?!

AND WAIT, WHAAAT?!!

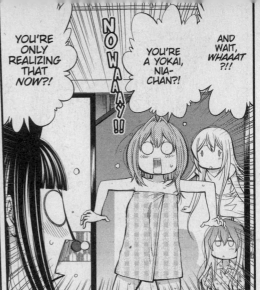

FIGURE IT OUT YET?

You're slow.

THAT'S WHAT YOU WERE TALKING ABOUT?!

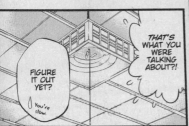

FLINCH

WHAT IS IT MEOW?!!

AHHH!!!

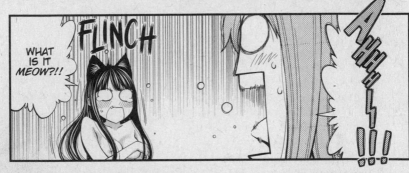

BUT WAIT, NIA-CHAN...

Those cat ears are so cute!

Your nose is bleeding too much, but...

DRIP DRIP DRIP

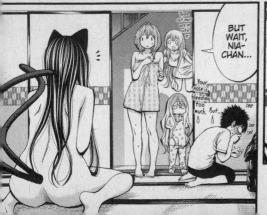

MAYBE IT'S NOT THAT YOU'RE SLOW... YOU'RE JUST DUMB.

Totally dumb.

I TOTALLY FORGOT ABOUT IT ONCE I SAW THE CATS...

COME TO THINK OF IT, I SAW YOU GOING TO THE CAT SHRINE!

I remember now!

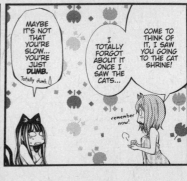

HOW...
DID YOU GET THOSE WOUNDS?
!
......
KIN
OH!
KIYUUU UU
TWIST TWIST

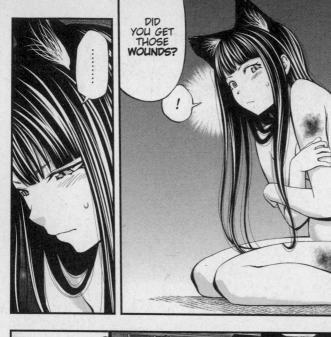

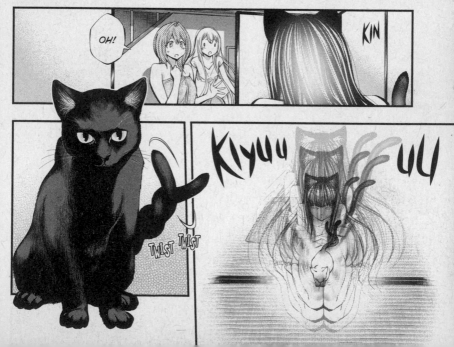

NIA-CHAN!
STAGGER STAGGER
!
GLARE...
RSTL...
NIA-CHAN ...
YOU'RE FINE BEING NAKED WHEN YOU'RE A CAT, HUH?!
LEAVE HER ALONE!
JEEZ.

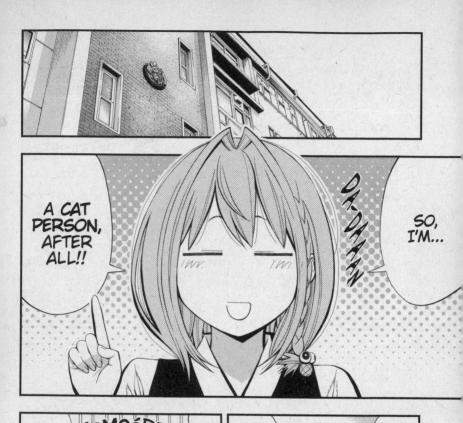

A CAT PERSON, AFTER ALL!!

DA-DAAAN

SO, I'M...

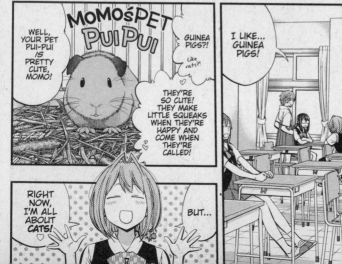

MOMO'S PET PUI PUI

WELL, YOUR PET PUI-PUI IS PRETTY CUTE, MOMO!

GUINEA PIGS?!

Like rats?!

I LIKE... GUINEA PIGS!

WHERE'S THIS COMING FROM?

Ha!

I PREFER DOGS!

THEY'RE SO CUTE! THEY MAKE LITTLE SQUEAKS WHEN THEY'RE HAPPY AND COME WHEN THEY'RE CALLED!

RIGHT NOW, I'M ALL ABOUT CATS!

BUT...

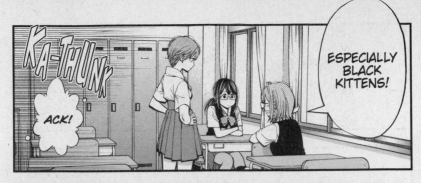

KA-THUNK!

ACK!

ESPECIALLY BLACK KITTENS!

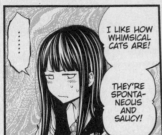

I LIKE HOW WHIMSICAL CATS ARE!

THEY'RE SPONTANEOUS AND SAUCY!

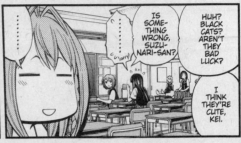

IS SOMETHING WRONG, SUZUNARI-SAN?

Curry...

HUH? BLACK CATS? AREN'T THEY BAD LUCK?

I THINK THEY'RE CUTE, KEI.

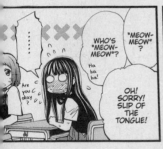

"MEOW-MEOW"?

WHO'S "MEOW-MEOW"?

Ha ha ha!

OH! SORRY! SLIP OF THE TONGUE!

Are you okay?

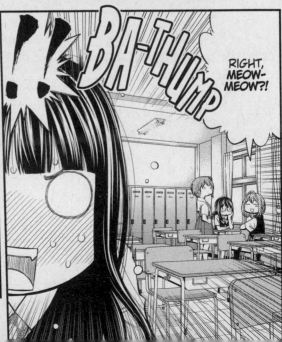

BA-THUMP

RIGHT, MEOW-MEOW?!

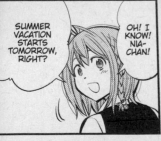

SUMMER VACATION STARTS TOMORROW, RIGHT?

OH! I KNOW! NIA-CHAN!

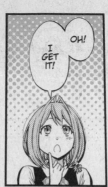

OH!

I GET IT!

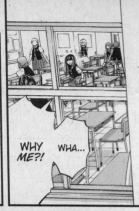

WHY ME?!

WHA...

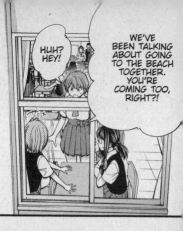

HUH? HEY!

WE'VE BEEN TALKING ABOUT GOING TO THE BEACH TOGETHER. YOU'RE COMING TOO, RIGHT?!

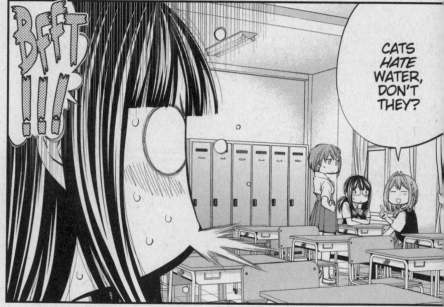

BFFT!!!

CATS *HATE* WATER, DON'T THEY?

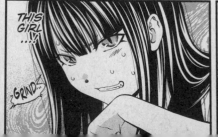

THIS GIRL...!

GRIND...

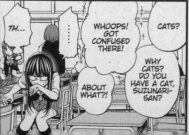

WHOOPS! GOT CONFUSED THERE!

CATS?

TH...

....

ABOUT WHAT?!

WHY CATS? DO YOU HAVE A CAT, SUZUNARI-SAN?

Aha ha ha ha!
See you!
Bye!
WHAT KIND OF GAME ARE YOU PLAYING?
ARE YOU THREATEN-ING ME?
AW, NO WAY! I'D NEVER DO THAT!
I'M JUST--

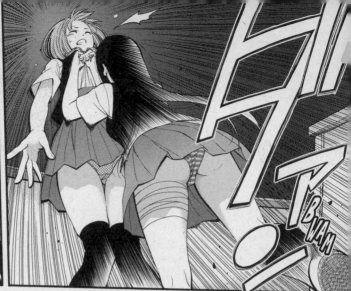

GAH
...!

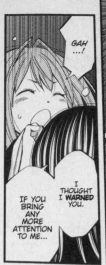

IF YOU BRING ANY MORE ATTENTION TO ME...

I THOUGHT I **WARNED** YOU.

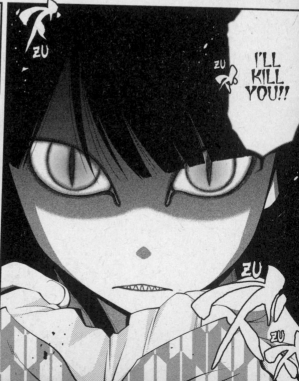

ZU

ZU

I'LL KILL YOU!!

ZU

ZU

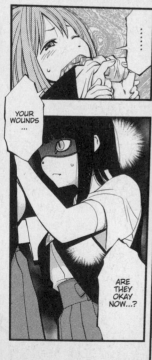

YOUR WOUNDS...

ARE THEY OKAY NOW...?

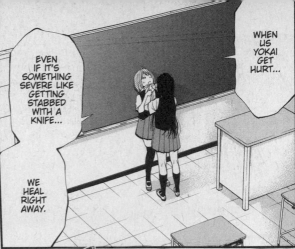

WHEN US YOKAI GET HURT...

EVEN IF IT'S SOMETHING SEVERE LIKE GETTING STABBED WITH A KNIFE...

WE HEAL RIGHT AWAY.

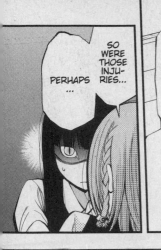

SO WERE THOSE INJU- RIES...

PERHAPS ...

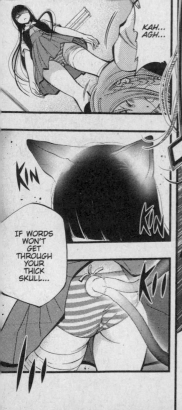

KAH... AGH...

KIN

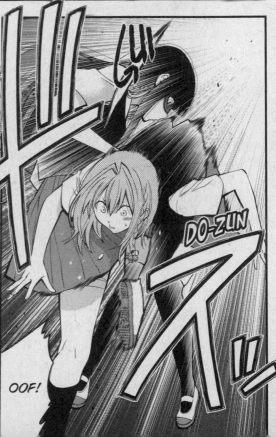

IF WORDS WON'T GET THROUGH YOUR THICK SKULL...

KIN

KIN

DO-ZUN

OOF!

NEKOMATA
THEN MAYBE A BEATING WILL!!
ZAAN

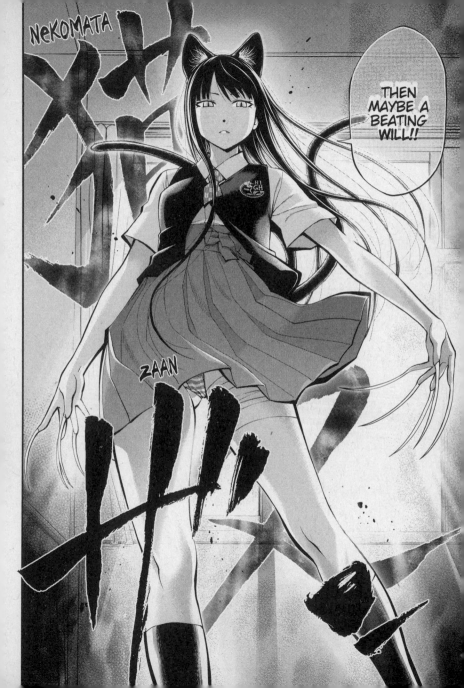

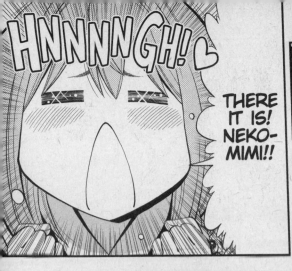

HNNNNNGH! ♡

THERE IT IS! NEKO-MIMI!!

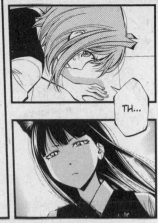

TH...

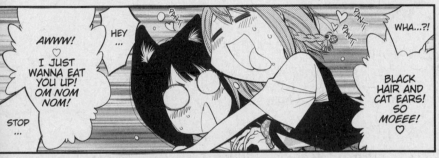

HEY...

AWWW! ♡ I JUST WANNA EAT YOU UP! OM NOM NOM!

STOP...

PAN!! PAN!!

WHA...?!

BLACK HAIR AND CAT EARS! SO MOEEE! ♡

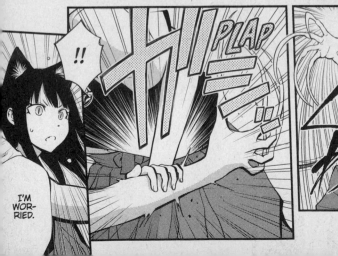

!!

TZ!! PLAP

I'M WORRIED.

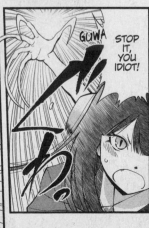

GUWA

STOP IT, YOU IDIOT!

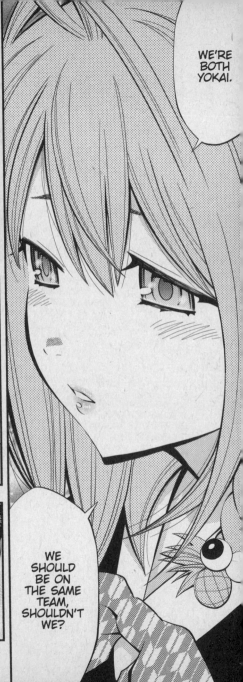

WE'RE BOTH YOKAI.

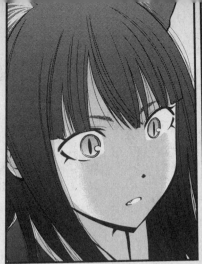

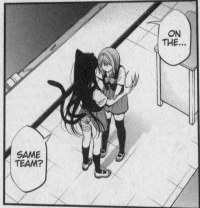

ON THE...

SAME TEAM?

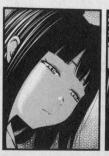

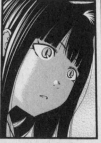

WE SHOULD BE ON THE SAME TEAM, SHOULDN'T WE?

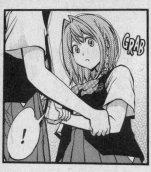

GRAB

!

DO-ZUN

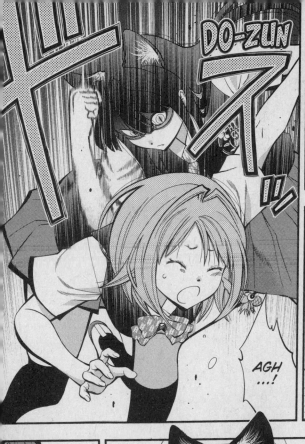

AGH
....!

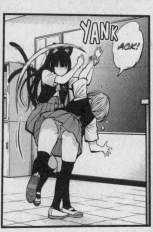

YANK

AOK!

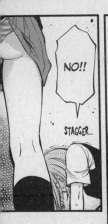

NO!!

STAGGER...

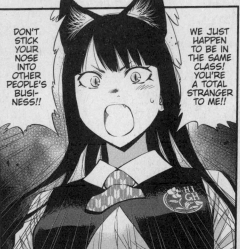

DON'T STICK YOUR NOSE INTO OTHER PEOPLE'S BUSINESS!!

WE JUST HAPPEN TO BE IN THE SAME CLASS! YOU'RE A TOTAL STRANGER TO ME!!

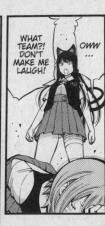

WHAT TEAM?! DON'T MAKE ME LAUGH!

OWW...

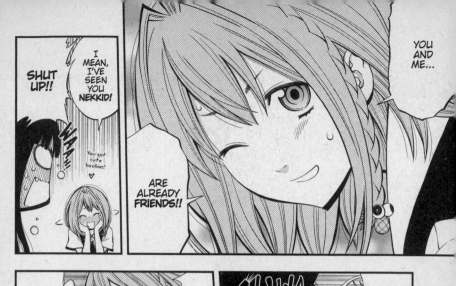

SHUT UP!!

I MEAN, I'VE SEEN YOU NEKKID!

WAA!!

You got cute boobies! ♥

ARE ALREADY FRIENDS!!

YOU AND ME...

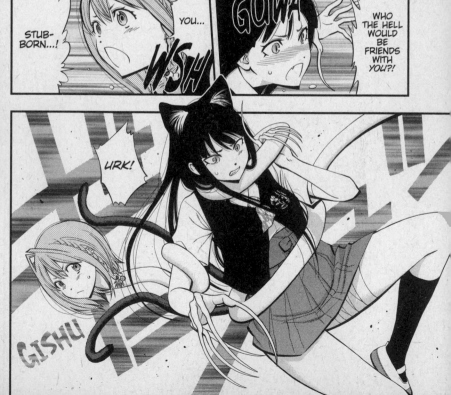

STUB-BORN...!

YOU...

WSH

GUWA

WHO THE HELL WOULD BE FRIENDS WITH YOU?!

URK!

GISHU

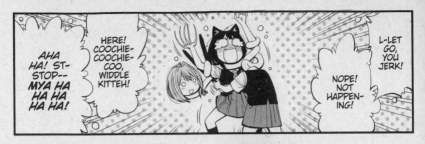

AHA HA! ST-STOP-- MYA HA HA HA HA HA!

HERE! COOCHIE-COOCHIE-COO, WIDDLE KITTEH!

L-LET GO, YOU JERK!

NOPE! NOT HAPPENING!

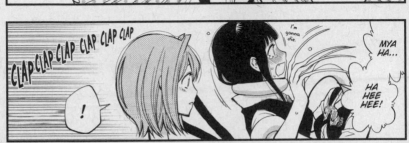

CLAP CLAP CLAP CLAP CLAP CLAP

!

I'm gonna die.

MYA HA...

HA HEE HEE!

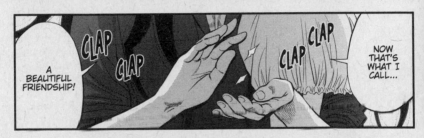

CLAP CLAP

CLAP CLAP

A BEAUTIFUL FRIENDSHIP!

NOW THAT'S WHAT I CALL...

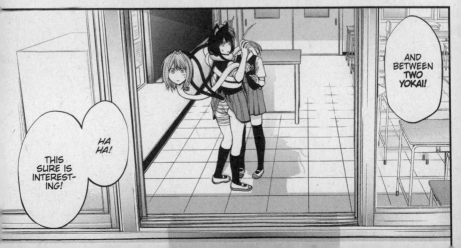

AND BETWEEN TWO YOKAI!

THIS SURE IS INTERESTING!

HA HA!

WHAT'S WRONG?
GO ON...
CONTINUE. PLEASE.
HIGH

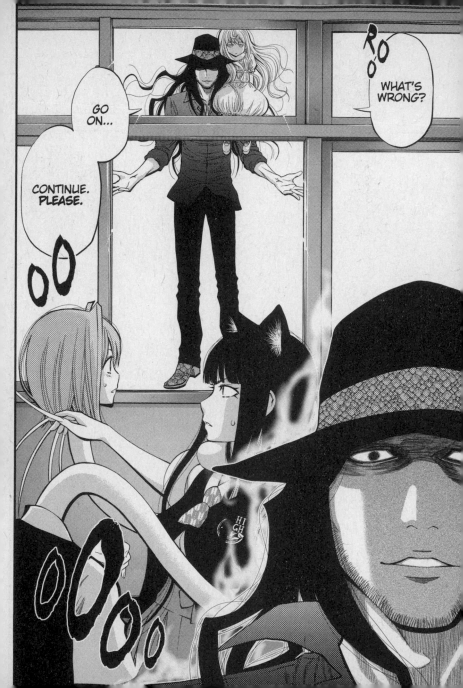

WHAT'S WRONG?
GO ON...
32
Pet (Meat Slave) ♥♪
CONTINUE. PLEASE.

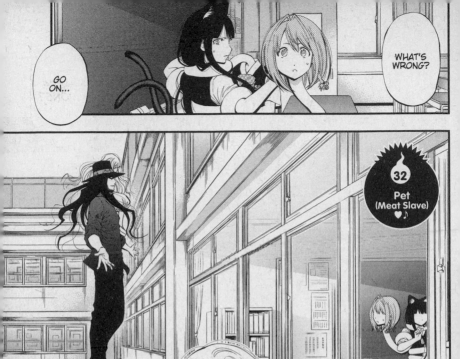

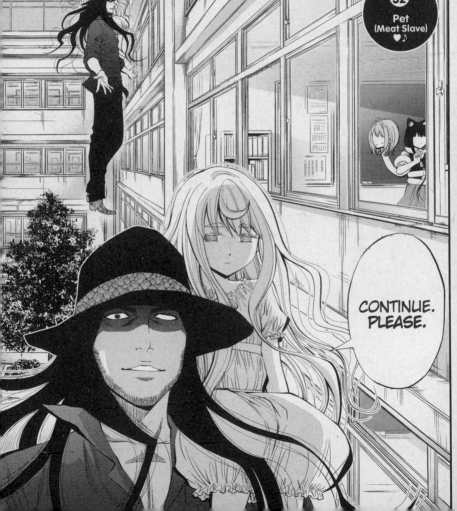

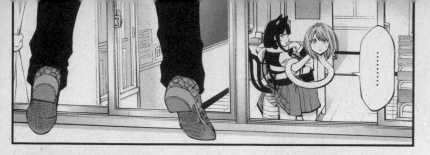

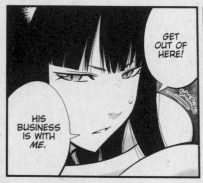

GET OUT OF HERE!

HIS BUSINESS IS WITH *ME.*

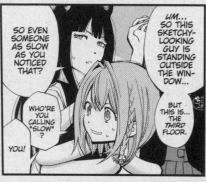

SO EVEN SOMEONE AS SLOW AS YOU NOTICED THAT?

WHO'RE YOU CALLING "SLOW"?

YOU!

UM... SO THIS SKETCHY-LOOKING GUY IS STANDING OUTSIDE THE WINDOW...

BUT THIS IS... THE *THIRD* FLOOR.

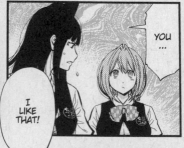

YOU ...

I LIKE THAT!

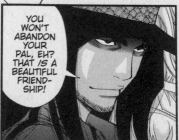

YOU WON'T ABANDON YOUR PAL, EH? THAT *IS* A BEAUTIFUL FRIENDSHIP!

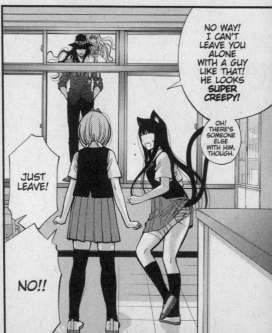

JUST LEAVE!

NO WAY! I CAN'T LEAVE YOU ALONE WITH A GUY LIKE THAT! HE LOOKS SUPER CREEPY!

OH! THERE'S SOMEONE ELSE WITH HIM, THOUGH.

NO!!

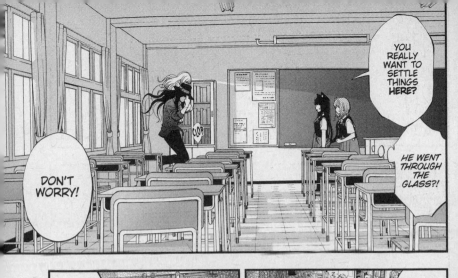

YOU REALLY WANT TO SETTLE THINGS HERE?

HE WENT THROUGH THE GLASS?!

DON'T WORRY!

CLOP

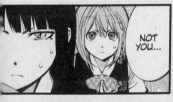

US FOUR ARE THE ONLY ONES AWAKE.

ZZZ...

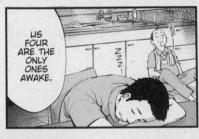

I PUT ALL THE HUMANS TO SLEEP.

ZZZ

NOT YOU...

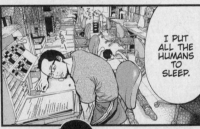

BE-SIDES...

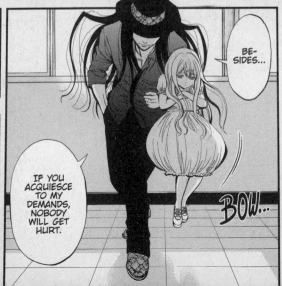

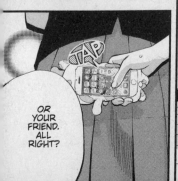

TAP

OR YOUR FRIEND. ALL RIGHT?

IF YOU ACQUIESCE TO MY DEMANDS, NOBODY WILL GET HURT.

BOW...

GIIIN
YOU'RE ...
DON
THE ONE WHO'S GONNA GET HURT!
BO-BAA

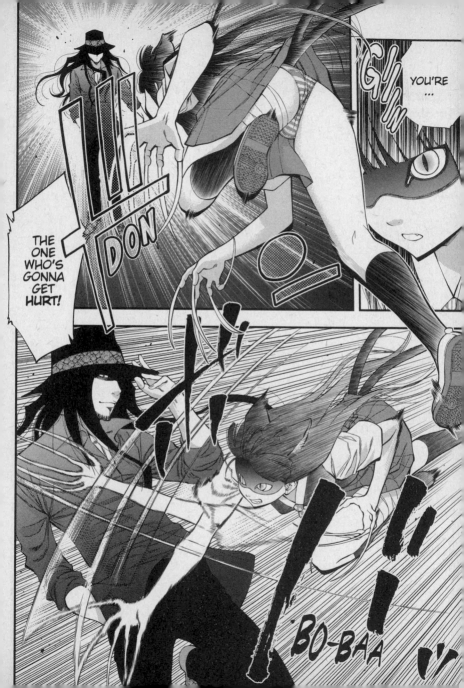

TON
TO
GRREOW!!
DO-SHU
SO CLOSE! ♪
NGH...

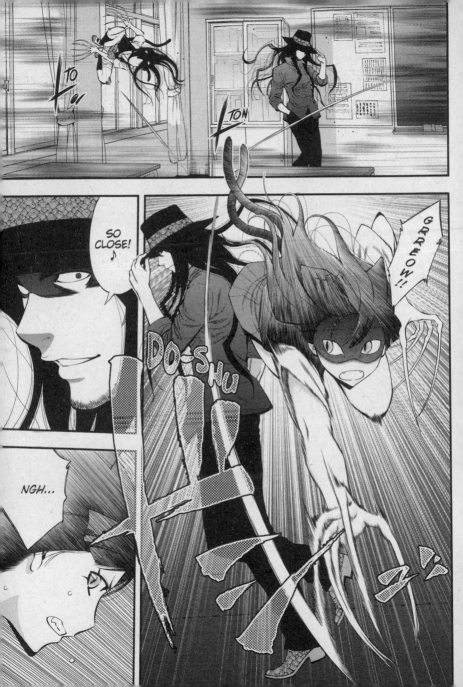

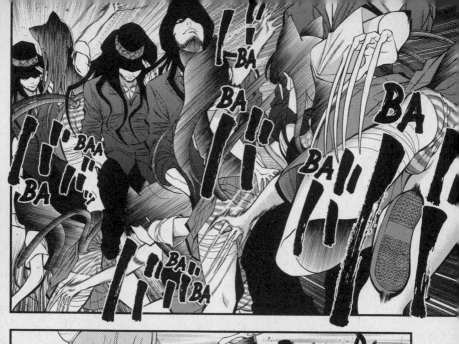

BA
BAA
BA
BA
BAII
BA
BAII
BA
BAII
BAII
BA

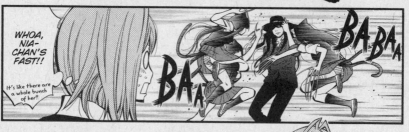

WHOA, NIA-CHAN'S FAST!!

It's like there are a whole bunch of her!!

BAA

BA-BAA

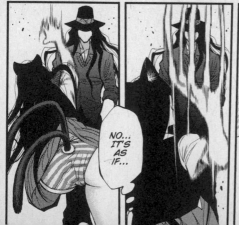

NO... IT'S AS IF...

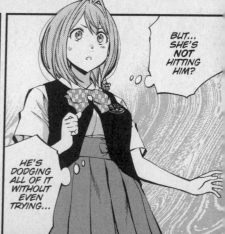

BUT... SHE'S NOT HITTING HIM?

HE'S DODGING ALL OF IT WITHOUT EVEN TRYING...

NIA-CHAN IS DELIBERATELY...
CHOOSING NOT TO HIT HIM.
FUWA...
!!
SUPA
NGH...
GYURUN
THERE!
KUI
HYUO

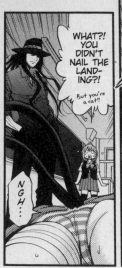

WHAT?! YOU DIDN'T NAIL THE LAND-ING?!

But you're a cat!!

NGH...

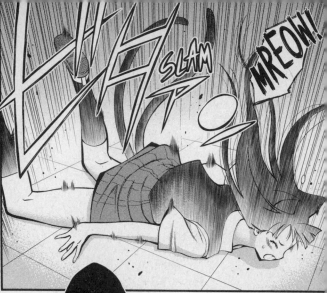

SLAM

MREOW!

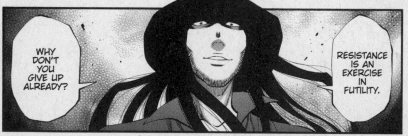

WHY DON'T YOU GIVE UP ALREADY?

RESISTANCE IS AN EXERCISE IN FUTILITY.

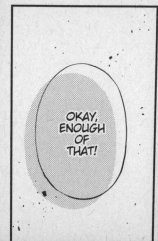

OKAY, ENOUGH OF THAT!

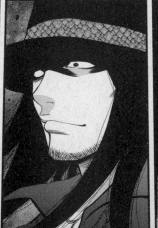

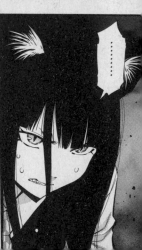

!
GISHU
HUH ?!
YOU...

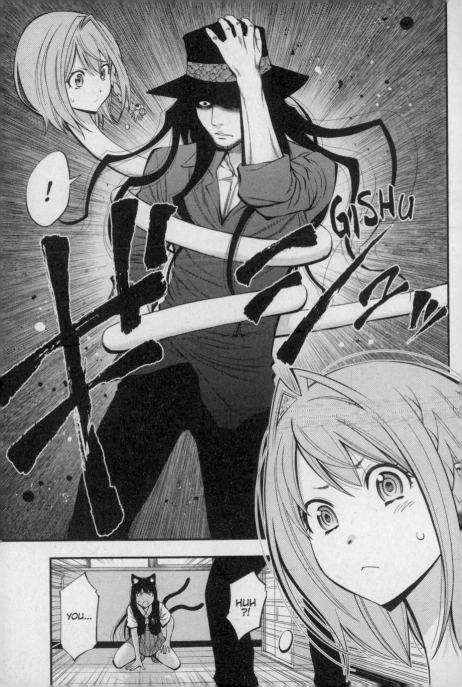

I SEE.
THAT'S TOO BAD...
WHAT THE HECK?
I'VE WRAPPED HIM UP TIGHT, BUT IT DOESN'T FEEL LIKE I'M SQUEEZ-ING HIM!
AM I NOT EVEN TOUCHING HIS BODY?!
!!
PAAN
GWAGH!
THA-THUD
AYA-TSUJI!!

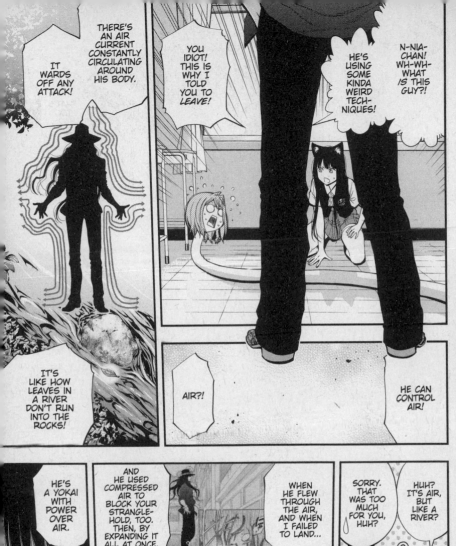

IT WARDS OFF ANY ATTACK!

THERE'S AN AIR CURRENT CONSTANTLY CIRCULATING AROUND HIS BODY.

YOU IDIOT! THIS IS WHY I TOLD YOU TO LEAVE!

HE'S USING SOME KINDA WEIRD TECHNIQUES!

N-NIA-CHAN! WH-WH-WHAT IS THIS GUY?!

IT'S LIKE HOW LEAVES IN A RIVER DON'T RUN INTO THE ROCKS!

AIR?!

HE CAN CONTROL AIR!

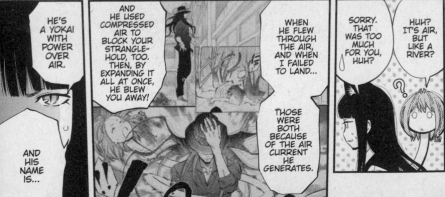

HE'S A YOKAI WITH POWER OVER AIR.

AND HIS NAME IS...

AND HE USED COMPRESSED AIR TO BLOCK YOUR STRANGLE-HOLD, TOO. THEN, BY EXPANDING IT ALL AT ONCE, HE BLEW YOU AWAY!

WHEN HE FLEW THROUGH THE AIR, AND WHEN I FAILED TO LAND...

THOSE WERE BOTH BECAUSE OF THE AIR CURRENT HE GENERATES.

SORRY. THAT WAS TOO MUCH FOR YOU, HUH?

HUH? IT'S AIR, BUT LIKE A RIVER?

GWO GWO
SORAGAMI!
GWO
GWO
I GROW WEARY OF THESE GAMES. TIME TO END THIS.
ROOO
HYOI

?
WHAT'S THIS?
FUWA...
RUN, YOU IDIOT!
EEEK!
BWAM
DO
GA
GAN
STOMP
UNG...

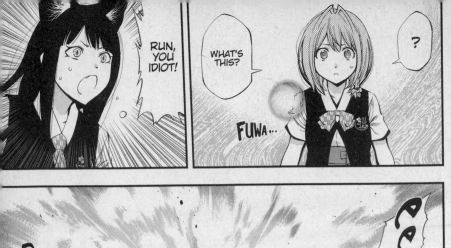

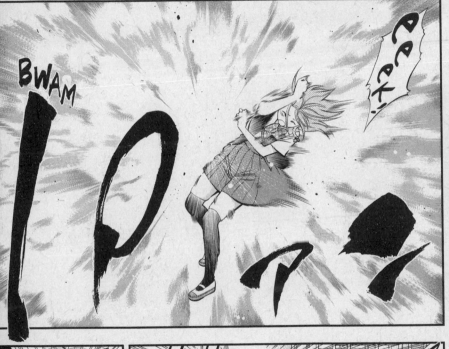

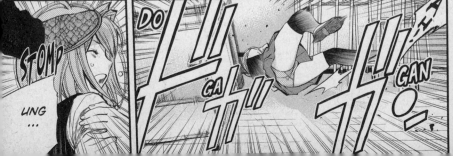

NOW WHAT WILL YOU DO?
YOUR FRIEND LIVES OR DIES, BASED ON YOUR RESPONSE.
GIVE UP AND BECOME MY PET!
KWOO
OOOH
UGH ...
P...
PET ?!
STRAIN STRAIN
YOU'VE GOTTA BE...
KIDDING ME.
THERE'S NO WAY...
I'D LET YOU DO THAT!
AYA-TSUJI...
HOW COULD I?!
MAKING NIA-CHAN...

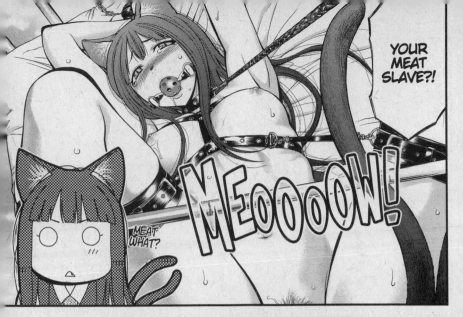

YOUR MEAT SLAVE?!

MEAT WHAT?

MEOOOOOW!

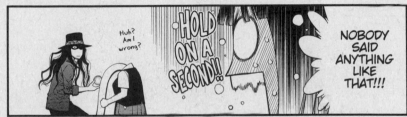

Huh? Am I wrong?

HOLD ON A SECOND!!

NOBODY SAID ANYTHING LIKE THAT!!!

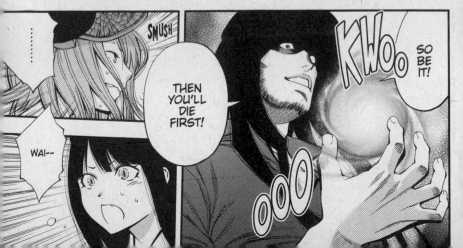

SMUSH

THEN YOU'LL DIE FIRST!

WAI--

KWOO

OOO

SO BE IT!

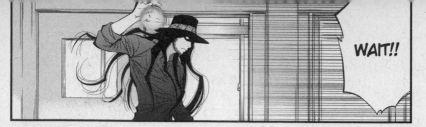

WAIT!!

NIA-CHA...

DON'T GET THE WRONG IDEA.

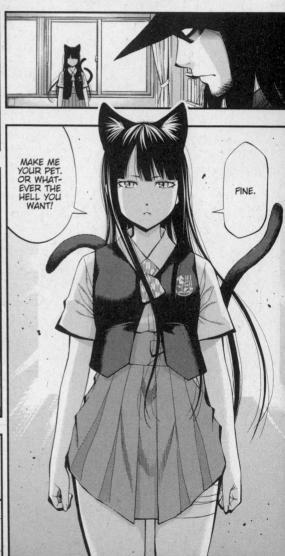

MAKE ME YOUR PET. OR WHATEVER THE HELL YOU WANT!

FINE.

I CHANGED MY MIND, THAT'S ALL.

I'M NOT DOING THIS FOR YOU.

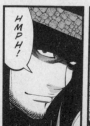

HMPH!

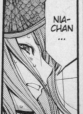

NIA-CHAN...

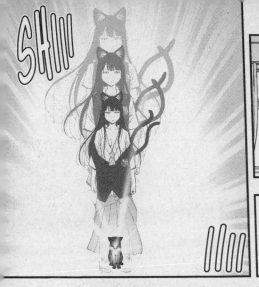

SHIIII

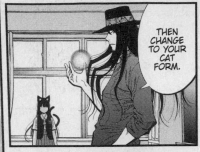

THEN CHANGE TO YOUR CAT FORM.

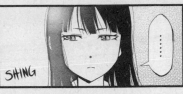

......

SHING

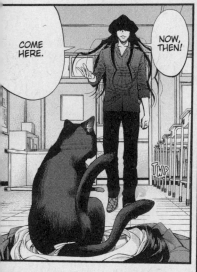

COME HERE.

NOW, THEN!

TWP

IIIIING...

RUSTLE...

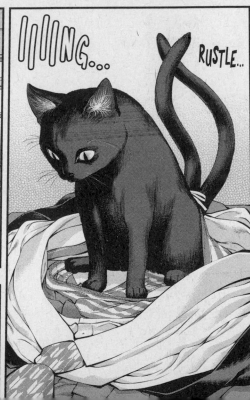

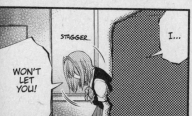

STAGGER

I...

WON'T LET YOU!

I ACTU-ALLY...
DIDN'T WANT TO SHOW THIS TO ANYONE...
BUT THIS IS A SPECIAL OCCASION!
ZU ZU...
I'LL SHOW YOU, YEP.
ZU ZU
MY...
KILLER MOVE!!
ZU
ZU

33
Tail Guard! ♪
I WON'T LET YOU MAKE NIA-CHAN YOUR PET!
I'LL SHOW YOU...
ZU
ZU
ZU
ZU
MY...
KILLER MOVE!!

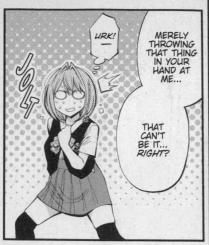

URK!

MERELY THROWING THAT THING IN YOUR HAND AT ME...

THAT CAN'T BE IT... *RIGHT?*

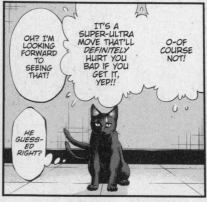

OH? I'M LOOKING FORWARD TO SEEING THAT!

IT'S A SUPER-ULTRA MOVE THAT'LL *DEFINITELY* HURT YOU BAD IF YOU GET IT, YEP!!

O-OF COURSE NOT!

HE GUESS-ED RIGHT?

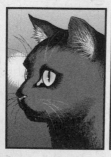

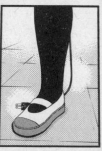

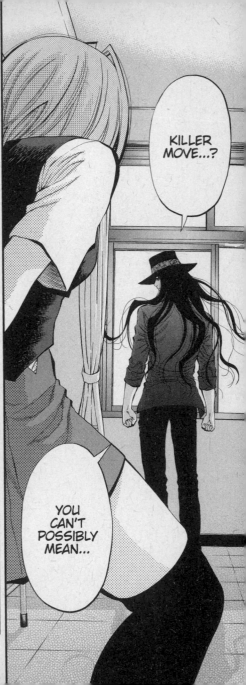

KILLER MOVE...?

YOU CAN'T POSSIBLY MEAN...

OH!
!
DASH
IT'S...
YOU'RE NOT GETTING AWAY.
KUI
HYUO
R
O
O
!
FWUA
OOO
NOW!
DO IT!

EEE-YAAHH!!!
LEAP
SHOCK
THE CAT TALKED!!!
HUH?!
GASHAAA
BUWA
BYUWAAA
?!
BUWA

A SMOKE SCREEN?!
NO, CHALK DUST!
SUPAAA
!
IF YOU CAN TALK, THEN JUST TELL ME! DON'T JUST BLURT WORDS OUT WITHOUT WARNING!
DO DO
DO
DO
I THOUGHT I WAS GONNA HAVE A HEART ATTACK! JEEZ! SERIOUSLY!
DANGLE
WOULD'VE BEEN MORE INTERESTING IF YOU HAD.
DO
HOW WOULD *THAT* BE INTER-ESTING?!

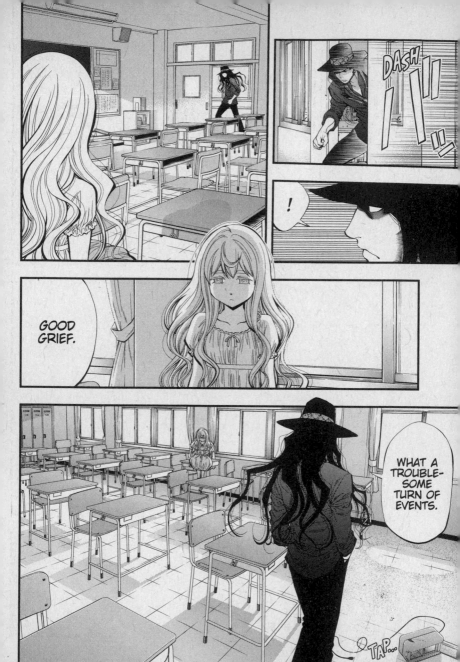

DASH

!

GOOD
GRIEF.

WHAT A
TROUBLE-
SOME
TURN OF
EVENTS.

TAP...

I HAVE AN IDEA!
JUST SUPPRESS YOUR YOKAI ENERGY FOR NOW!
FINE, NOW PUT ME DOWN!
I can run by myself!
UP IS BETTER!
WAIT... HEY! WHERE ARE YOU GOING?!
IF WE'RE RUNNING AWAY, YOU SHOULD BE GOING DOWN!
TAP TAP
TAP
THEY'VE SUP-PRESSED THEIR YOKAI ENERGIES TO HIDE, HUH?
UP?
TAP...

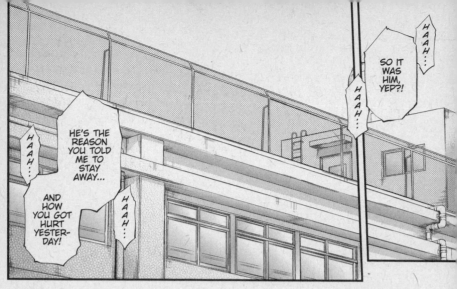

SO IT WAS HIM, YEP?!

HAAH...

HAAH...

HE'S THE REASON YOU TOLD ME TO STAY AWAY...

AND HOW YOU GOT HURT YESTERDAY!

HAAH...

HAAH...

WHAT THE HECK?!

HE SAID HE WANTS TO SHOW ME OFF.

THAT'S WHY?!

HE WANTS ME AS HIS PET BECAUSE TWIN-TAILS ARE RARE.

SHHH!

You're talking too loud!

NOBODY SAID ANYTHING ABOUT SEX SLAVES!

HAAH...

WHY DOES THAT GUY WANT TO MAKE YOU HIS MEAT SLAVE, NIA-CHAN?

HAAH...

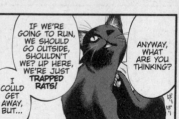

IF WE'RE GOING TO RUN, WE SHOULD GO OUTSIDE, SHOULDN'T WE? UP HERE, WE'RE JUST TRAPPED RATS!

I COULD GET AWAY, BUT...

ANYWAY, WHAT ARE YOU THINKING?

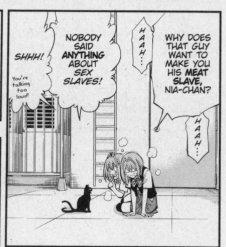

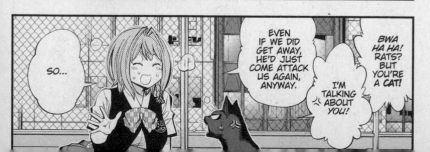

SO...

EVEN IF WE DID GET AWAY, HE'D JUST COME ATTACK US AGAIN, ANYWAY.

I'M TALKING ABOUT YOU!

BWA HA HA! RATS? BUT YOU'RE A CAT!

WE'LL FINISH HIM OFF NOW!
WHA ...?
HOW STUPID ARE YOU?! THERE'S NO WAY WE CAN BEAT HIM!
YOU DON'T KNOW THAT UNTIL YOU TRY!
LISTEN...
LIKE I SAID BEFORE, HE ALWAYS HAS WIND CURRENTS RUNNING AROUND HIS BODY.
IT'S LIKE HE'S WEARING ARMOR MADE OF AIR.
WHAT'S MORE, THAT ATTACK HE HIT YOU WITH BEFORE...
RUN, YOU IDIOT!
WAS AN AIR BULLET HE CREATES BY COMPRESSING AIR. AT IMPACT, HE EXPANDS THE AIR AGAIN TO CREATE AN EXPLOSION.
BWAM
SINCE THEY'RE MADE OF AIR, THEY'RE INVISIBLE!
JUST HOW ARE YOU SUPPOSED TO BEAT AN OPPONENT WITH INVISIBLE WEAPONS AND ARMOR YOU CAN'T HIT--
IT'S OKAY!

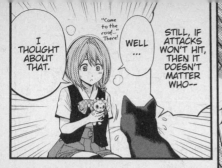

I THOUGHT ABOUT THAT.

"Come to the roof..." There!

WELL...

STILL, IF ATTACKS WON'T HIT, THEN IT DOESN'T MATTER WHO--

I'VE CALLED FOR BACKUP!

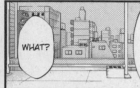

WHAT?

IF AN ATTACK IS HEAVIER THAN THE AIRFLOW, THEN I FIGURE HE COULDN'T PUSH IT AWAY, RIGHT?

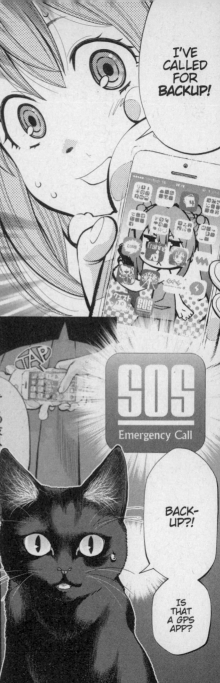

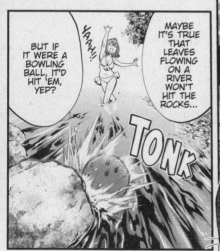

YAAH!!

BUT IF IT WERE A BOWLING BALL, IT'D HIT 'EM, YEP?

MAYBE IT'S TRUE THAT LEAVES FLOWING ON A RIVER WON'T HIT THE ROCKS...

TONK

TAP

SOS
Emergency Call

BACK-UP?!

IS THAT A GPS APP?

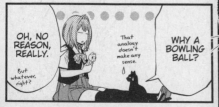

OH, NO REASON, REALLY.

But whatever, right?

That analogy doesn't make any sense.

WHY A BOWLING BALL?

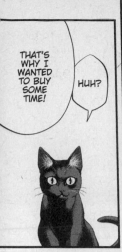

THAT'S WHY I WANTED TO BUY SOME TIME!

HUH?

WHO CAN HIT LIKE THAT!

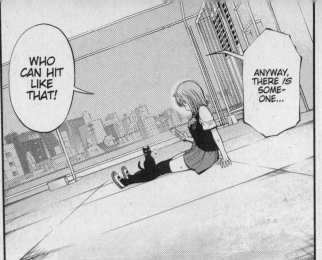

ANYWAY, THERE *IS* SOME-ONE...

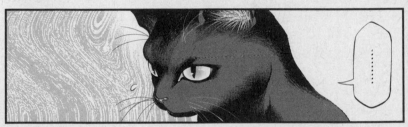

....

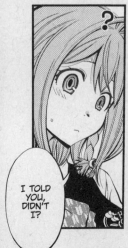

I TOLD YOU, DIDN'T I?

?

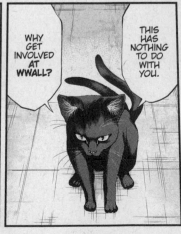

WHY GET INVOLVED AT WWALL?

THIS HAS NOTHING TO DO WITH YOU.

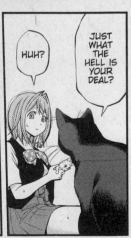

HUH?

JUST WHAT THE HELL IS YOUR DEAL?

BECAUSE WE'RE FRIENDS!
FRIENDS...
SHE'S ...
AGAIN ...
OH! THEY'RE COMING NOW!
OKAY, THEN WILL YOU GO BACK TO YOUR HUMAN FORM NOW?
HUH?
YOU NEED TO BE READY TO FIGHT!
YOU CAN'T HELP US LIKE THAT!
WHAT?
HEY, HOLD ON A SECOND!

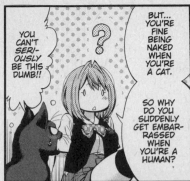

YOU CAN'T SERI-OUSLY BE THIS DUMB!!

BUT... YOU'RE FINE BEING NAKED WHEN YOU'RE A CAT.

SO WHY DO YOU SUDDENLY GET EMBAR-RASSED WHEN YOU'RE A HUMAN?

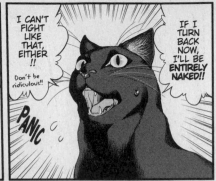

I CAN'T FIGHT LIKE THAT, EITHER!!

Don't be ridiculous!!

PANIC

IF I TURN BACK NOW, I'LL BE ENTIRELY NAKED!!

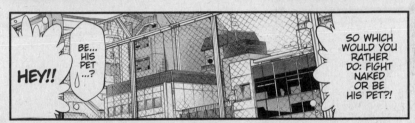

HEY!!

BE... HIS PET ...?

SO WHICH WOULD YOU RATHER DO: FIGHT NAKED OR BE HIS PET?!

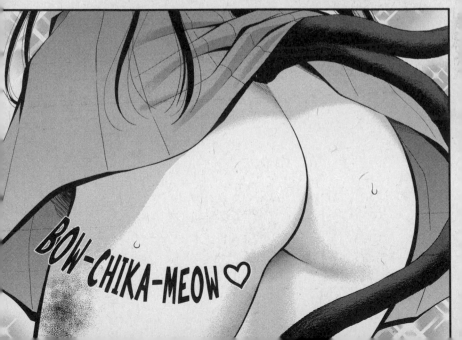

BOW-CHIKA-MEOW ♡

WAAAH!
HOW ...
AM I SUPPOSED TO FIGHT IN THIS?!
It's too embarrassing!
IT'S NOT MUCH, I KNOW.
REALLY FEELS LIKE THE MAX DIFFICULTY SETTING, HUH?
Ha ha...
FIDGET
FIDGET
BUT STILL, IT'S BETTER THAN FIGHTING COMMANDO LIKE YOU, NIA-CHAN!
HEY!
PEEK♡
TAIL GUARD!!
CURL♡
TAIL?
THAT'S NOT FAIR!!
Then give me back my skirt!
NYOOO!!
DON'T FLIP UP MY SKIRT, YOU JERK!!

BA
GA
GAAN
GAGAN
GAN
GARARA
NOT HERE, EITHER.
THERE'S NO INDICATION THAT THEY RAN OUTSIDE.
WHERE ARE THEY HIDING? ARE THEY TRYING TO BUY TIME?
!
TWITCH
WHAT IS THIS...
PRESENCE I SENSE?
I FEEL A STRANGE YOKAI ENERGY!!

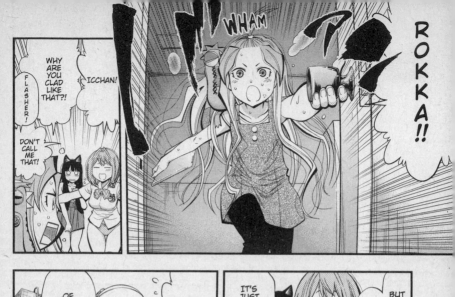

WHY ARE YOU CLAD LIKE THAT?!

FLASHER!

ICCHAN!

DON'T CALL ME THAT!

ROKKA!!

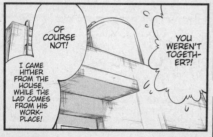

OF COURSE NOT!

I CAME HITHER FROM THE HOUSE, WHILE THE LAD COMES FROM HIS WORKPLACE!

YOU WEREN'T TOGETHER?!

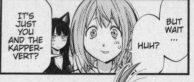

IT'S JUST YOU AND THE KAPPERVERT?

HUH?

BUT WAIT...

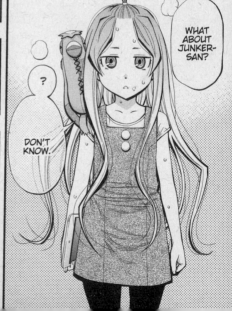

WHAT ABOUT JUNKERSAN?

?

DON'T KNOW.

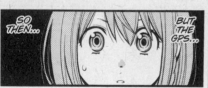

SO THEN...

BUT THE GPS...

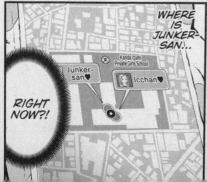

WHERE IS JUNKERSAN...

RIGHT NOW?!

Junkersan♥

Kanda Izumi Private Girls School

Icchan♥

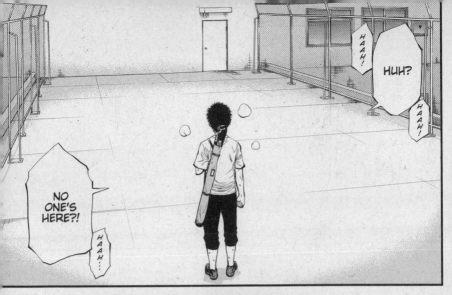

HAAH!

HUH?

HAAH!

NO ONE'S HERE?!

HAAH...

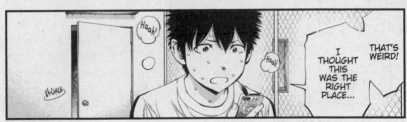

Haah!

Haah!

THAT'S WEIRD!

I THOUGHT THIS WAS THE RIGHT PLACE...

KA-CHACK

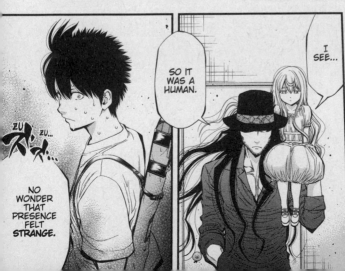

ZU... ZU...

NO WONDER THAT PRESENCE FELT STRANGE.

SO IT WAS A HUMAN.

I SEE...

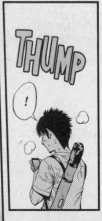

THUMP

!

ZU
ZU
YOU HAVE...
PSYCHIC POWERS, DON'T YOU?
ZU
WHAT THE HELL...
IS THIS GUY?!
ZU
ZU
ZU
OH, CRAP!

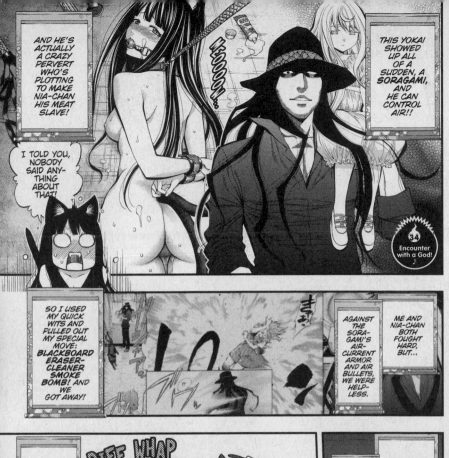

AND HE'S ACTUALLY A CRAZY PERVERT WHO'S PLOTTING TO MAKE NIA-CHAN HIS MEAT SLAVE!

THIS YOKAI SHOWED UP ALL OF A SUDDEN, A SORAGAMI, AND HE CAN CONTROL AIR!!

I TOLD YOU, NOBODY SAID ANY-THING ABOUT THAT!

34
Encounter with a God!

SO I USED MY QUICK WITS AND PULLED OUT MY SPECIAL MOVE: BLACKBOARD ERASER-CLEANER SMOKE BOMB! AND WE GOT AWAY!

AGAINST THE SORA-GAMI'S AIR-CURRENT ARMOR AND AIR BULLETS, WE WERE HELP-LESS.

ME AND NIA-CHAN BOTH FOUGHT HARD, BUT...

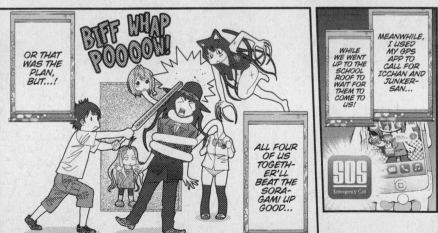

OR THAT WAS THE PLAN, BUT...!

BIFF WHAP POOOOOW!

ALL FOUR OF US TOGETH-ER'LL BEAT THE SORA-GAMI UP GOOD...

WHILE WE WENT UP TO THE SCHOOL ROOF TO WAIT FOR THEM TO COME TO US!

MEANWHILE, I USED MY GPS APP TO CALL FOR ICCHAN AND JUNKER-SAN...

SOS
Emergency Call

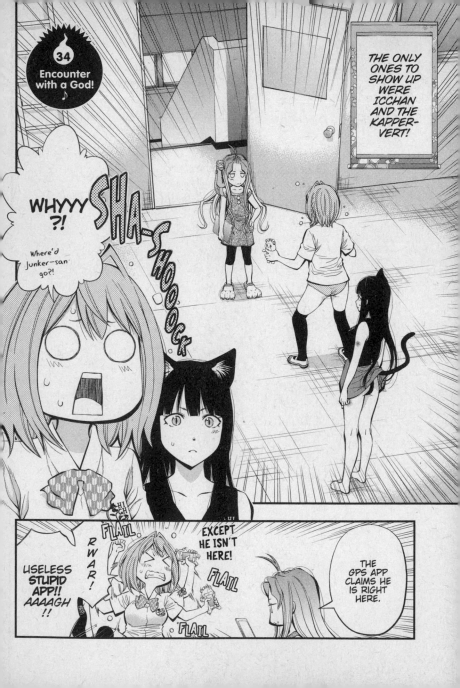

THE ONLY ONES TO SHOW UP WERE ICCHAN AND THE KAPPER-VERT!

WHYYY?!

Where'd Junker-san go?!

SHA-SHOOOOK

EXCEPT HE ISN'T HERE!

RWAR!

FLAIL

FLAIL

FLAIL

USELESS STUPID APP!! AAAAGH!!

THE GPS APP CLAIMS HE IS RIGHT HERE.

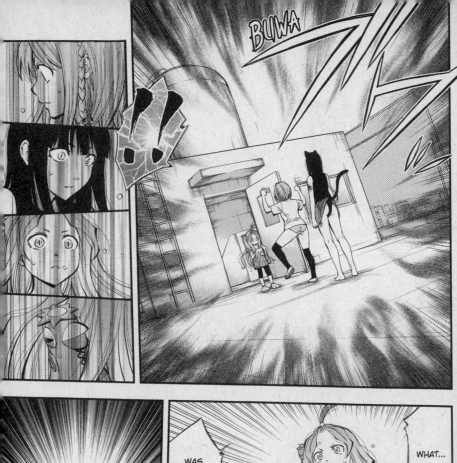

BUWA

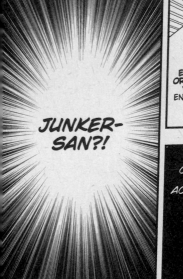

JUNKER-SAN?!

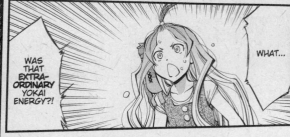

WAS THAT EXTRAORDINARY YOKAI ENERGY?!

WHAT...

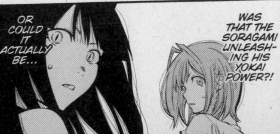

OR COULD IT ACTUALLY BE...

WAS THAT THE SORAGAMI UNLEASHING HIS YOKAI POWER?!

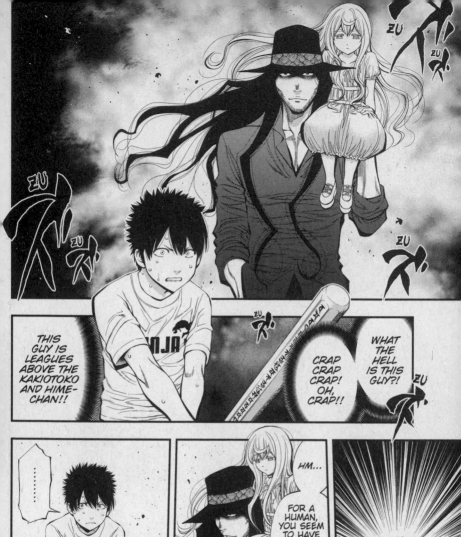

THIS GUY IS LEAGUES ABOVE THE KAKIOTOKO AND HIME-CHAN!!

CRAP CRAP CRAP! OH, CRAP!!

WHAT THE HELL IS THIS GUY?!

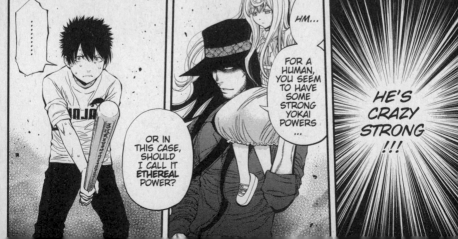

HM...

FOR A HUMAN, YOU SEEM TO HAVE SOME STRONG YOKAI POWERS...

OR IN THIS CASE, SHOULD I CALL IT ETHEREAL POWER?

HE'S CRAZY STRONG !!!

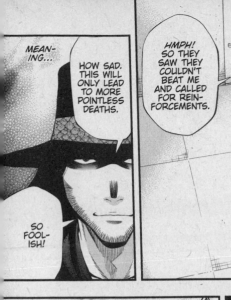

MEAN-ING...

HOW SAD. THIS WILL ONLY LEAD TO MORE POINTLESS DEATHS.

SO FOOL-ISH!

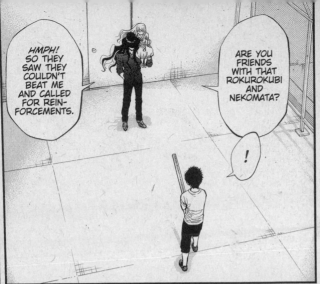

HMPH! SO THEY SAW THEY COULDN'T BEAT ME AND CALLED FOR REIN-FORCEMENTS.

ARE YOU FRIENDS WITH THAT ROKUROKUBI AND NEKOMATA?

!

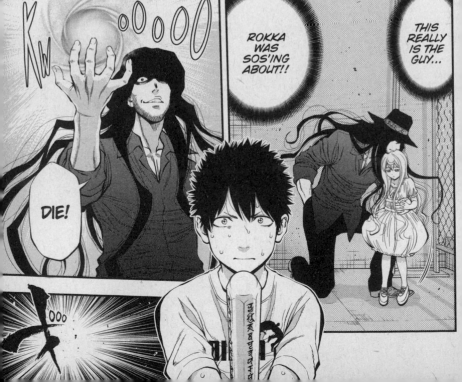

DIE!

ROKKA WAS SOS'ING ABOUT!!

THIS REALLY IS THE GUY...

PASHU
BOH!!
?!!

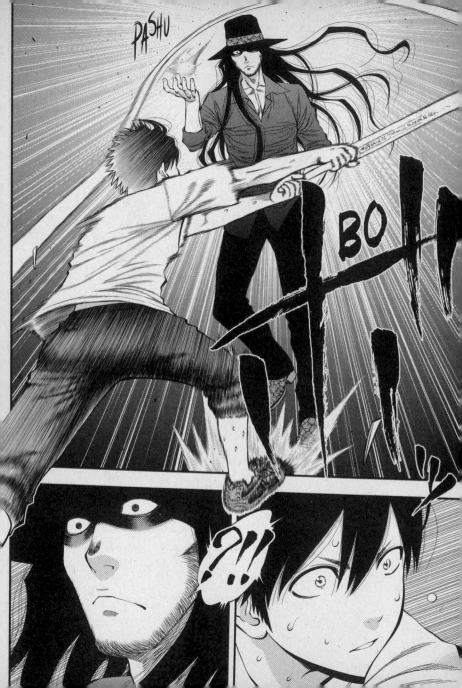

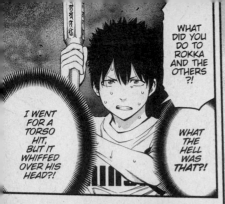

WHAT DID YOU DO TO ROKKA AND THE OTHERS?!

WHAT THE HELL WAS THAT?!

I WENT FOR A TORSO HIT, BUT IT WHIFFED OVER HIS HEAD?!

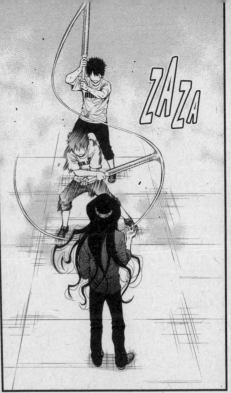

ZA ZA

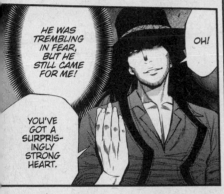

HE WAS TREMBLING IN FEAR, BUT HE STILL CAME FOR ME!

OH!

YOU'VE GOT A SURPRIS- INGLY STRONG HEART.

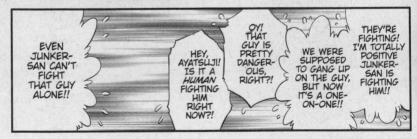

EVEN JUNKER-SAN CAN'T FIGHT THAT GUY ALONE!!

HEY, AYATSUJI! IS IT A HUMAN FIGHTING HIM RIGHT NOW?!

OY! THAT GUY IS PRETTY DANGER-OUS, RIGHT?!

WE WERE SUPPOSED TO GANG UP ON THE GUY, BUT NOW IT'S A ONE-ON-ONE!!

THEY'RE FIGHTING! I'M TOTALLY POSITIVE JUNKER-SAN IS FIGHTING HIM!!

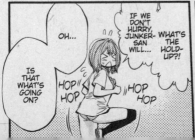

OH...

IS THAT WHAT'S GOING ON?

IF WE DON'T HURRY, JUNKER-SAN WILL...

WHAT'S THE HOLD-UP?!

HOP HOP

HOP HOP

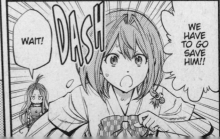

WAIT!

DASH

WE HAVE TO GO SAVE HIM!!

IF THE LAD IS ALREADY THERE...
THEN WE SHOULD PLAN OUR ENTRANCE.
HUH?
PAUSE...
LET'S...
HAVE A LITTLE FUN!
ROO
WHAT IS THIS FEELING?
IT WAS LIKE THAT WHEN I TRIED A BODY HIT, TOO.
SOMETHING FEELS REALLY OFF!!
I CAN TELL THAT HE'S CRAZY STRONG...
AND ALSO THAT HE'S BEEN GOING AFTER ROKKA AND THE OTHERS...
BUT... WHAT IS THIS?!
I FEEL LIKE I'M FORGETTING SOMETHING IMPORTANT!!
FUWA...

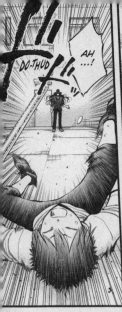

DO-THUD

AH ....!

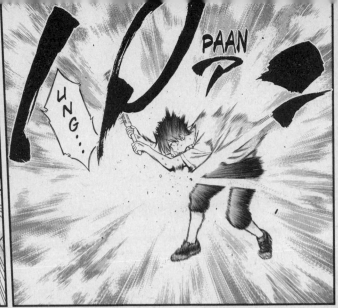

UNG...

PAAN

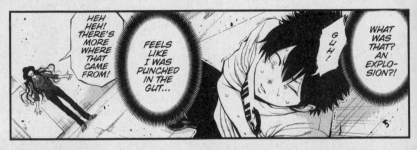

HEH HEH! THERE'S MORE WHERE THAT CAME FROM!

FEELS LIKE I WAS PUNCHED IN THE GUT...

GUH!

WHAT WAS THAT? AN EXPLOSION?!

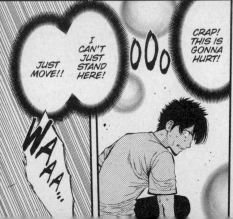

I CAN'T JUST STAND HERE!

JUST MOVE!!

OOOo

CRAP! THIS IS GONNA HURT!

WAAA...

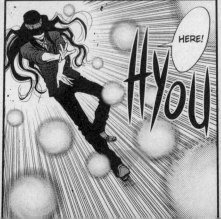

HERE!

HYOU

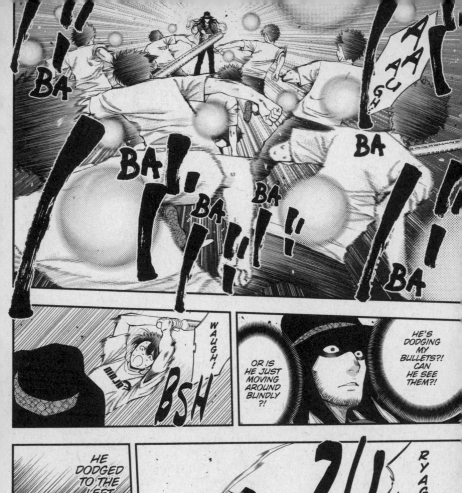

BA

BA

BA

BA

BA

BA

BA

A AU GH

WAUGH!

BSH

OR IS HE JUST MOVING AROUND BLINDLY?!

HE'S DODGING MY BULLETS?! CAN HE SEE THEM?!

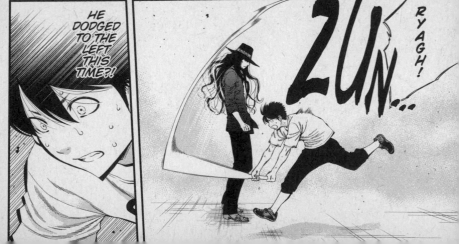

HE DODGED TO THE LEFT THIS TIME?!

ZUN...

RYAGH!

URGH...
PAAN
AH!
NINJA
NOT AGAIN...
YOU'RE INTERESTING...
BUT...
IT'S OVER!
DON
DO
DO

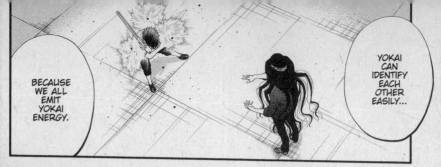

BECAUSE WE ALL EMIT YOKAI ENERGY.

YOKAI CAN IDENTIFY EACH OTHER EASILY...

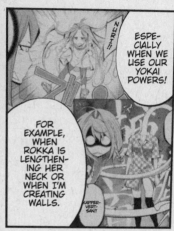

ESPE-CIALLY WHEN WE USE OUR YOKAI POWERS!

FOR EXAMPLE, WHEN ROKKA IS LENGTHEN-ING HER NECK OR WHEN I'M CREATING WALLS.

NURI!!

KAPPER-VERT-SAN!!

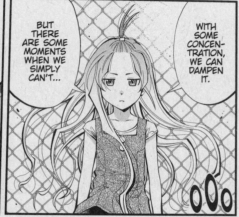

BUT THERE ARE SOME MOMENTS WHEN WE SIMPLY CAN'T...

WITH SOME CONCEN-TRATION, WE CAN DAMPEN IT.

ESPECIALLY IF THEY'RE IN THE MIDDLE OF A FIGHT WITH ANOTHER YOKAI!

IF THERE'S OTHER YOKAI CLOSE BY...

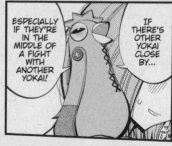

CORRECT!

HM!

TAP

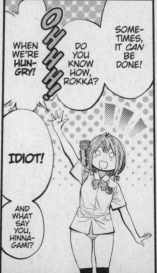

WHEN WE'RE HUN-GRY!

OHHH!!

DO YOU KNOW HOW, ROKKA?

SOME-TIMES, IT CAN BE DONE!

IDIOT!

AND WHAT SAY YOU, HINNA-GAMI?

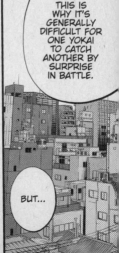

THIS IS WHY IT'S GENERALLY DIFFICULT FOR ONE YOKAI TO CATCH ANOTHER BY SURPRISE IN BATTLE.

BUT...

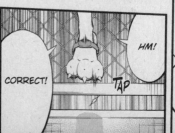

THE GPS APP...
ISN'T BROKEN!
BSH
WE ARE IN THE SAME SPOT!
Kanda Izumi Private Girls School
Junker-san♥
Icchan♥
ONLY...

ON DIFFERENT LEVELS!
DON
CRASHING WALL DEATH-PRESS !!!!!
THE FULL FORCE OF MY WALL, ABOUT A TON OF PRESSURE, BEARING DOWN ON YOU!!
IF YOU CAN WARD THIS AWAY...
NGH...
OH?
THEN GIVE IT YOUR BEST SHOT!!

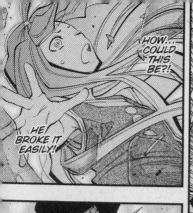

HOW...
COULD
THIS
BE?!

HE
BROKE IT
EASILY!!

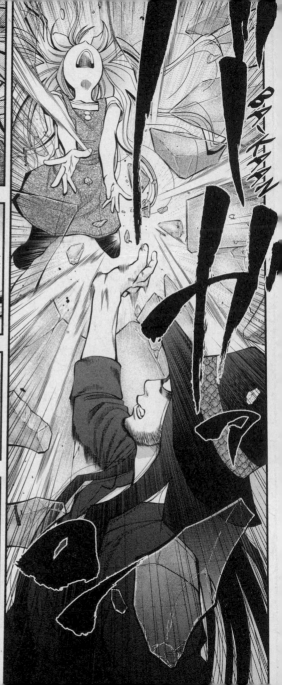

BA
KAAN

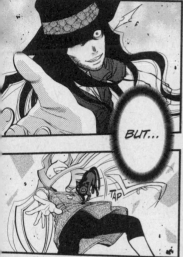

BUT...

TAP

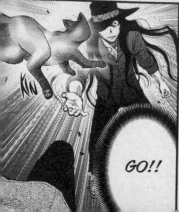

KIN

GO!!

CAT!!!
ZA

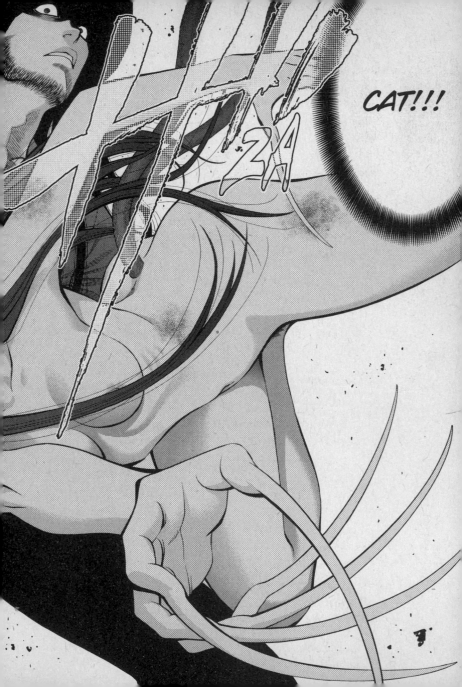

NO! HE DODGED IT!!
FWA HA!
TOO BAD!

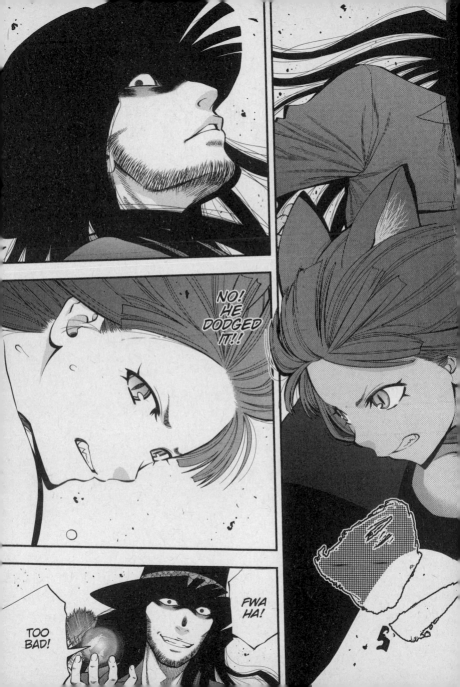

BA-WACK

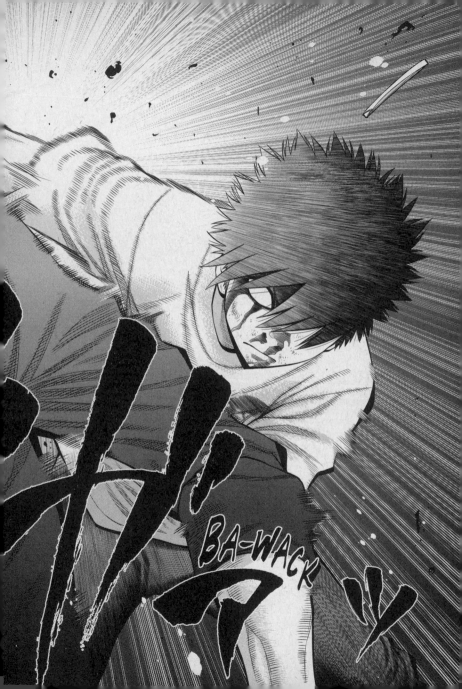

Extra: As Yatsuki vs. Soragami is going on...

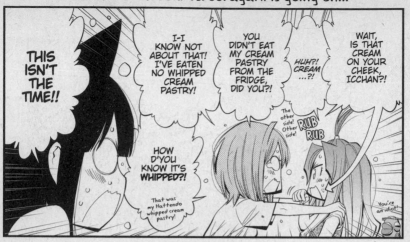

Nanao's Question

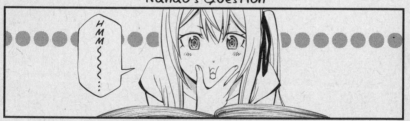

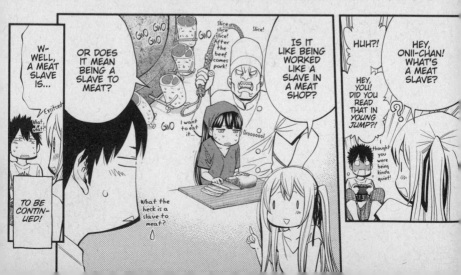

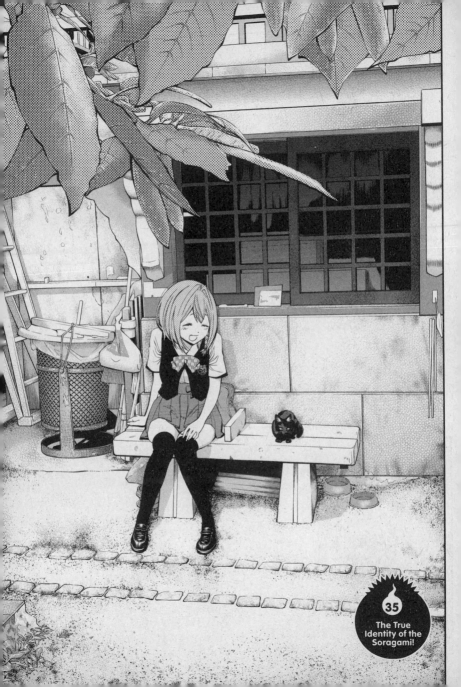

35
The True
Identity of the
Soragami!

BA-WACK

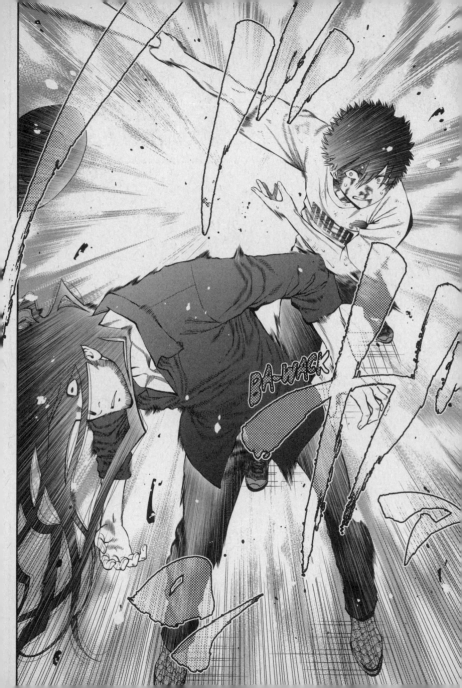

GGH...
AUGH...
STAGGER...
IT WORKED?!
HIS AIR ARMOR HAS WEAKENED!!
NOW!! HAVE AT HIM, ALL AT ONCE!!
N-NAKED...
SPLFF SPLFFT
D-DON'T LOOK AT ME!!
S-S-S-S-SORRY...
CUT THAT OUT!
ATTACK NOW, WHILE HE'S WEAK!!
......
YOU... FILTHY...

KRACK!!
!!
CRUMBLE...
IT'S EASY TO CATCH HIM BY SURPRISE IF YOU USE SOMETHING WITHOUT ANY YOKAI POWER IN IT!

THIS IS MY KILLER MOVE! BOWLING ATTACK!!
IT MAY JUST BE A PHYSICAL ATTACK, BUT IT HURTS!
I DON'T FEEL PAIN, MYSELF.
Though I can be startled!
I CREATED AN OPENING...
FOR JUST AN IN-STANT, AT LEAST!!
GO!!
NIA-CHAN!!
TAKE THIS!!!

DO
DO
DARK CAT SCRATCH COMBO!!
NINE!!!
DO
DO

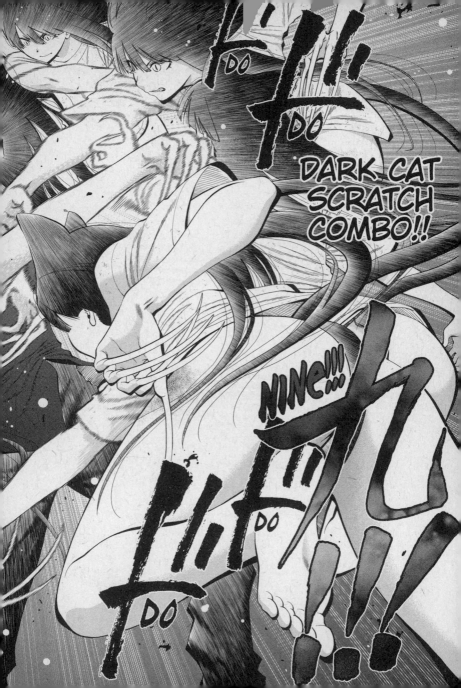

DO
DO
DO
YOU...
SCUM...
DIE!
CASHU
TUMP

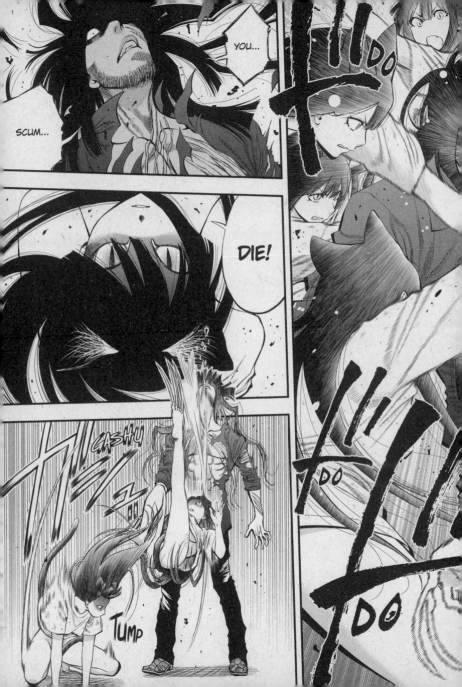

TEN!!!
STRIPPED TREE
GA-ZON

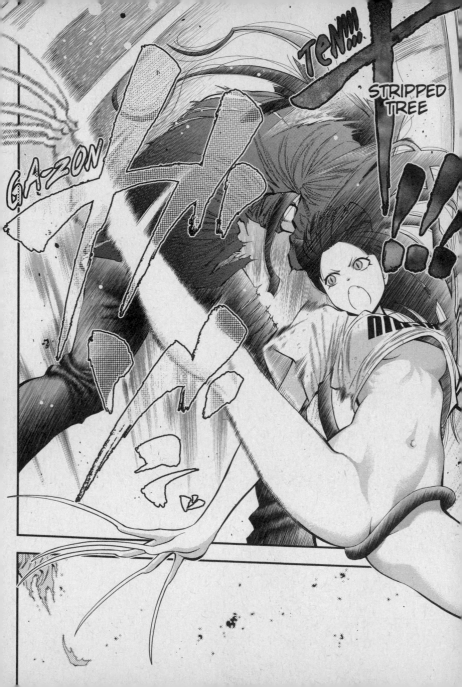

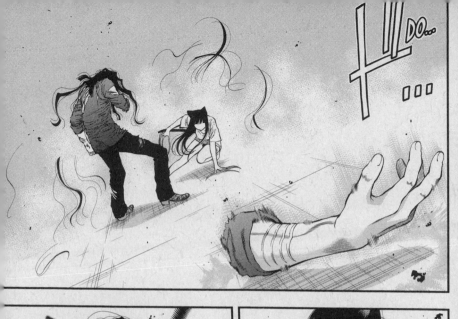

HU DO...
...

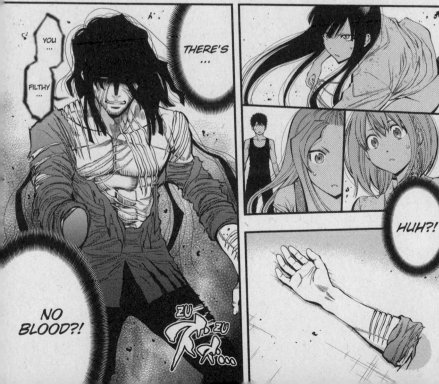

YOU
...

FILTHY
...

THERE'S
...

HUH?!

NO
BLOOD?!

ZU
ZU ZU
ZU...

YOU FILTHY SCUM!!!
DON
WAH!!!
UNFORGIVABLE!!
YOU BASE YOKAI, YOU SQUALID INSECTS!!
YOU SCUM SHOULD PROSTRATE YOURSELVES AT MY FEET!!
ROO
PIKI
YOU...
OOO
PIKIKI
YOU GARBAGE!!
BIKI
OO

I'M NOT GOING TO MAKE YOU MY PET ANYMORE...
I'M GOING TO KILL YOU!!
I'LL WIPE YOU OUT... UNTIL THERE'S NOT A SINGLE DROP OF BLOOD, NOT A SINGLE SPECK OF DUST LEFT!!!
ROOO
OOO
BO
BO
WHOA!
BYUN
DASH
KA
KA
KA
Nun!
DASH!!

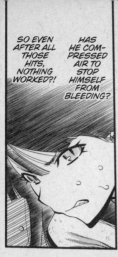

SO EVEN AFTER ALL THOSE HITS, NOTHING WORKED?!

HAS HE COMPRESSED AIR TO STOP HIMSELF FROM BLEEDING?

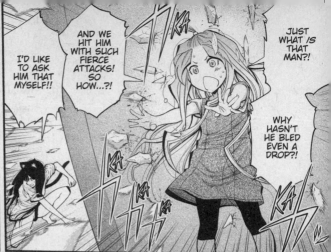

I'D LIKE TO ASK HIM THAT MYSELF!!

AND WE HIT HIM WITH SUCH FIERCE ATTACKS! SO HOW...?!

JUST WHAT *IS* THAT MAN?!

WHY HASN'T HE BLED EVEN A DROP?!

KA

KA

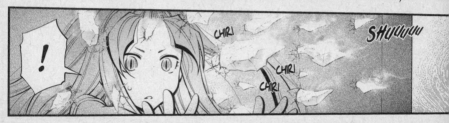

!

CHIRI

CHIRI

CHIRI

SHUUUU

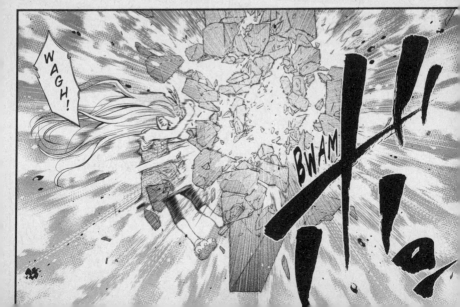

WAGH!

BWAM

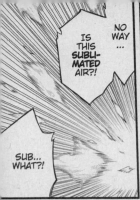

IS THIS SUBLIMATED AIR?!

NO WAY...

SUB... WHAT?!

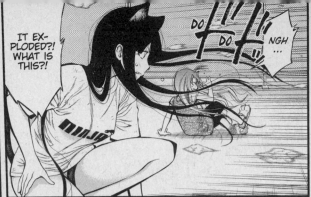

IT EXPLODED?! WHAT IS THIS?!

DO!!

DO!!

NGH...

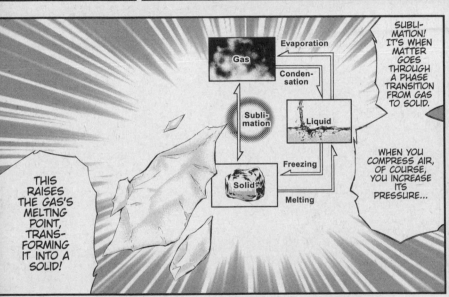

SUBLIMATION! IT'S WHEN MATTER GOES THROUGH A PHASE TRANSITION FROM GAS TO SOLID.

Gas

Evaporation

Condensation

Sublimation

Liquid

Freezing

Solid

Melting

WHEN YOU COMPRESS AIR, OF COURSE, YOU INCREASE ITS PRESSURE...

THIS RAISES THE GAS'S MELTING POINT, TRANSFORMING IT INTO A SOLID!

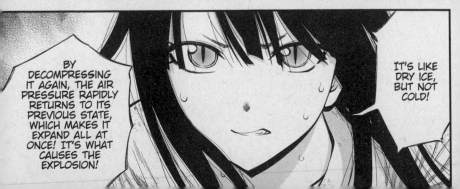

BY DECOMPRESSING IT AGAIN, THE AIR PRESSURE RAPIDLY RETURNS TO ITS PREVIOUS STATE, WHICH MAKES IT EXPAND ALL AT ONCE! IT'S WHAT CAUSES THE EXPLOSION!

IT'S LIKE DRY ICE, BUT NOT COLD!

SORA-GAMI...
ROO
OO
OO
I HAD NO IDEA HE WAS *THIS* POWERFUL!
OOO
SORA-GAMI...
YOU SAY?
CAT!
DID YOU JUST SAY, "SORA-GAMI"?!
WHAT ABOUT IT? THAT'S HIS NAME!
Don't call me "cat"!
OO
OOO
SORA-GAMI...
SO HE'S SORA-GAMI?!
OOO

IF THAT IS SO, THEN...
NO MATTER HOW MANY OF US BAND TOGETHER, WE CAN'T BEST HIM!
WE'VE MADE ENEMIES OF AN *INCREDIBLY* POWERFUL YOKAI!
ROO
SORAGAMI IS JUST AN ALIAS!
HIS TRUE NAME IS...

OO
DAITENGU
!!!
OO
IROO

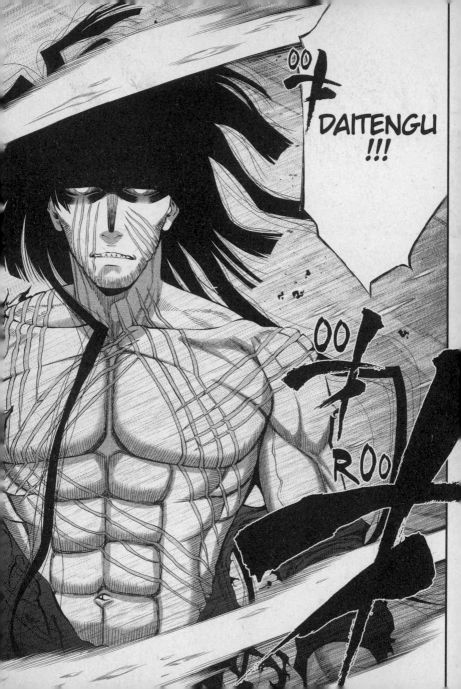

OO
OO
DAI...
TENGU...
BYUWA
GA-KUIN
!
BON
BO
I DUNNO ...
IF YOU'RE A SORAGAMI OR SOME KINDA TENGU OR WHAT...

YOU SAY YOU'RE GONNA KILL US?!
OR CALL THEM PETS OR INSECTS OR WHATEVER... I'M NOT HERE FOR THAT!!
ROO
BUT IF YOU'RE GONNA TALK SHIT ABOUT MY FRIENDS...
OOO
I'M NOT GONNA LET YOU!!!
OO
OO

TENGU.

THE FIRST SIGHTING OF A TENGU IS SAID TO BE THE AMAKITSUNE RECORDED IN NIHON SHOKI, IN THE FEBRUARY OF THE NINTH YEAR OF THE JOMEI EMPEROR (637 AD), BUT THAT IS DIFFERENT FROM THE TENGU DESCRIBED HERE, AND IS BELIEVED TO BE A SHOOTING STAR THAT SHOT FROM EAST TO WEST, MAKING A GREAT BOOMING NOISE AS IT WENT.

THEY SAY THAT WHEN A GROSSLY ARROGANT BUDDHIST ASCETIC DIES, HE IS DOOMED TO BECOME A TENGU. TENGU, BY NATURE, ARE FRIGHTENING, CAUSING GREAT STORMS IN THE MOUNTAINS AND ABDUCTING PEOPLE. ON THE OTHER OTHER HAND, THEY'RE ALSO OFTEN WORSHIPED AS SPIRITS OR GODS OF THE MOUNTAIN, AND ARE SAID TO WATCH OVER MOUNTAIN ASCETICS.

OFTEN DEPICTED AS ASCETICS WITH RED FACES AND LONG NOSES, IT WAS BELIEVED THAT TENGU TYPICALLY LIVED IN THE MOUNTAINS, CAUSING A VARIETY OF STRANGE PHENOMENA WITH THEIR SUPERNATURAL POWERS.

STORIES OF THIS YOKAI ABOUND IN EVERY REGION OF JAPAN.

BUT YOU SAY YOU'LL KILL US?

SOME KINDA TENGU OR WHAT...

I DUNNO IF YOU'RE ...

I'M NOT GONNA LET YOU!!
ZU
36
I Want to Save You...! ♪
ZU
ARE YOU EVEN CAPABLE...
ZU
HUMAN ?!
ZU

ROO
TAKE THIS!
BO
TENGU THROWING STONES.. HAIL!!
HUP!
DASH DASH
URK ... Nuri...
DON
BABA
KA KA KA KA KA KA KA KA

NGH!
IT'S NO USE FROM THIS DISTANCE!
I HAVE TO GET CLOSER!!
GRIND
BWAM
WHOA !!
BA-BWAM
DAMN IT!
HIS ATTACKS ARE COMING TOO HARD, AND I CAN'T EVEN GET CLOSE!
HAAH...
HAAH...
AND WHAT'S MORE...
EVEN IF I COULD GET CLOSE, THAT WHIRLWIND...!
HOW DO I GET THROUGH THAT?!
ROO
HMPH!
YOU CAN'T DEFEAT ME BY RUNNING AWAY!
NGH ...
HAAH...

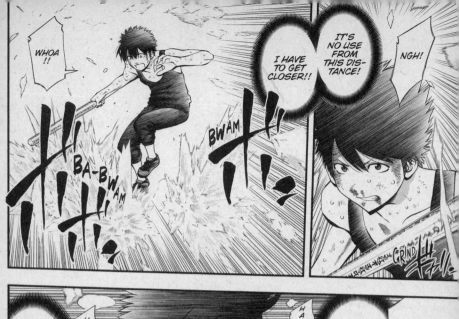

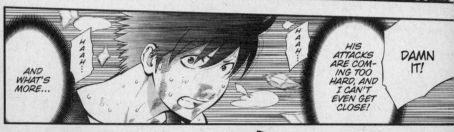

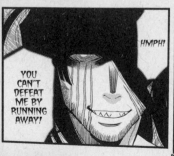

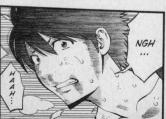

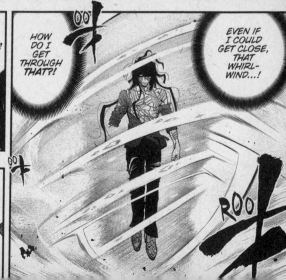

ARE HIS YOKAI POWERS INFINITE?!
AT THIS RATE, WE'LL EXHAUST OURSELVES!!
WHOA ...
DAMN IT!
WHAT DO WE DO?!
BA-BWAM
HEY!
?!
LISTEN TO ME!
WHA ...?!
WHAT ?!
WHAT ARE YOU TALKING ABOUT?!
I CAN'T DO THAT!
YOU'RE THE ONLY ONE WHO CAN DO IT!
AND THAT'S THE ONLY WAY WE'RE GETTING THROUGH THIS!
I DON'T UNDERSTAND!
WHAT'S THE POINT OF DOING THAT?!
GAGH!!
NO TIME TO TALK ABOUT IT!

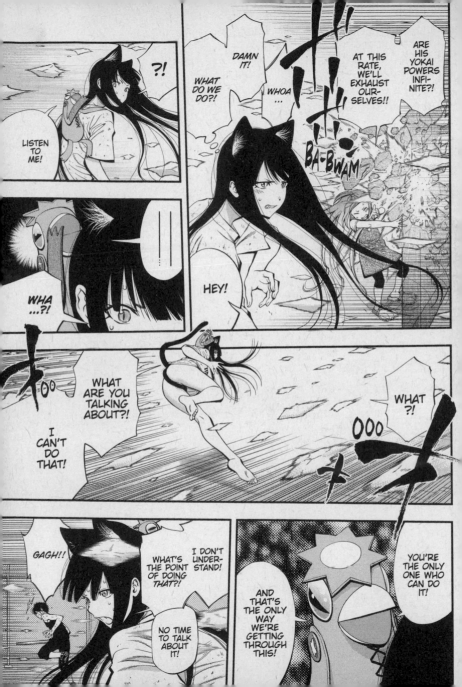

AH...
BA-BWAM
GAH!
LAD!
CHIRI CHIRI CHIRI
BA-DON
GYAGH!
ZAAA
!!

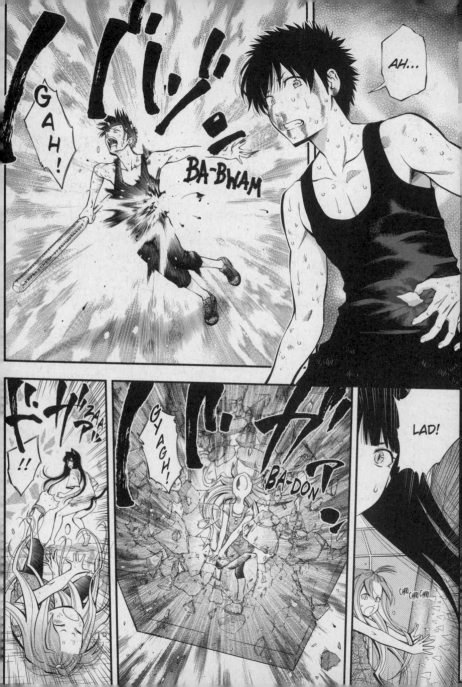

NGH ...
AH ...
UGH ...
WH--
WHAT SHOULD I DO...?
HEH HEH HEH...
ARE THOSE TWO DEAD ALREADY?
YOU'LL BE NEXT, CAT...
AND AFTER THAT, THE ROKURO-KUBI!
......
I'M...
NOT DEAD!

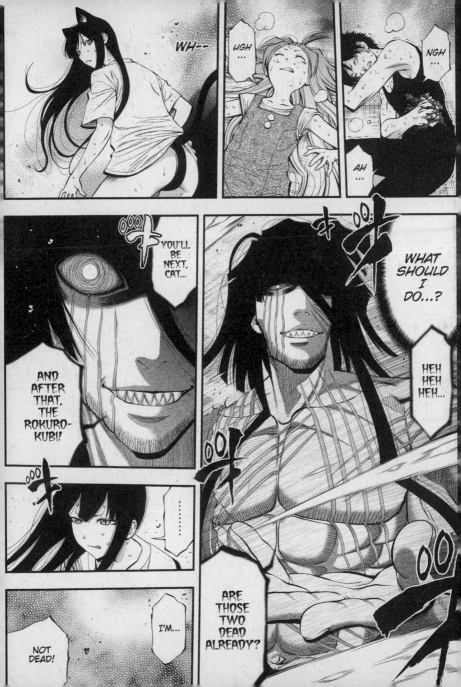

Haah
I SAID, I'M NOT...
ZU
Haah
GONNA LET YOU, DIDN'T I?
ZU
ZU
ZU
HEY...
THAT'S ENOUGH!
WHAT IS THE DEAL WITH YOU GUYS?!
YOU CAME ONLY BECAUSE AYATSUJI CALLED YOU HERE, RIGHT?!
WHY WOULD ANY OF YOU CARE ABOUT WHAT HAPPENS TO ME?!
'CAUSE...
I CAN'T HELP IT.
I MEAN, I'VE GOTTEN TO KNOW YOU.
HUH?

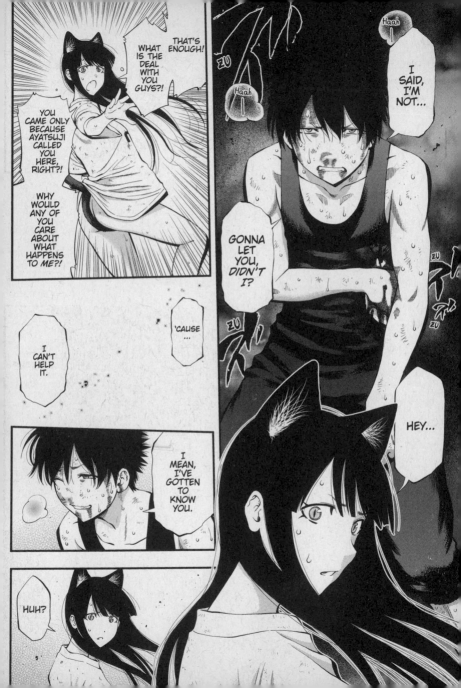

I'M NOT...
SOME BIG DAMN HERO.
AND I DON'T HAVE SOME SPECIAL SENSE OF JUSTICE OR WHATEVER.
NGH...
AND MAYBE...
IF YOU WERE SOME STRANGER, I MIGHT'VE RUN AWAY.
BUT...
NOW I'VE GOTTEN TO KNOW YOU.
YOU'RE...
ROKKA'S FRIEND, RIGHT?
WHAT I...

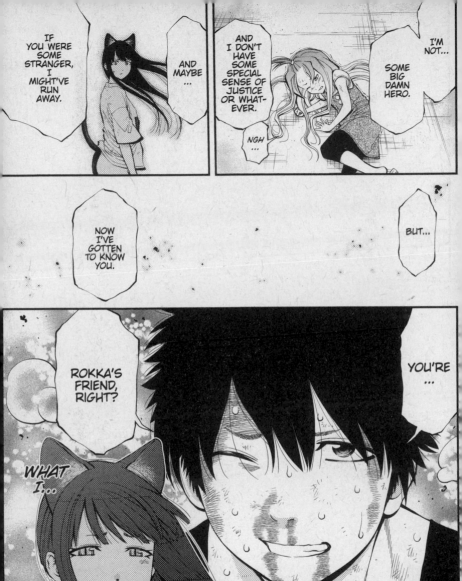

WHAT I CAN DO IS...
ZA...
ROOO
WHAT'S WRONG?
ARE YOU HERE TO BEG FOR YOUR LIFE?
......
THAT'S RIGHT!
DO WHAT YOU WANT WITH ME. KILL ME OR MAKE ME YOUR PET...
BUT THEY'VE GOT NOTHING TO DO WITH THIS.
LET THEM GO!
CAT...
HEY, HOLD ON--
NGH!
IT'S OKAY.

THIS IS MY CHOICE.
OOO
ROO
IF...
IF I COULD HAVE MET ALL OF YOU EAR-LIER...
OOO
WAIT --!
KWOOOO
SO BE IT.
PIKI
PIKI
BIKI
DIE!
OOO...
...
OR...
IF I HAD...

NOOO—!!!
JOLT
AYA-TSUJI!
SHUU...
NINJA

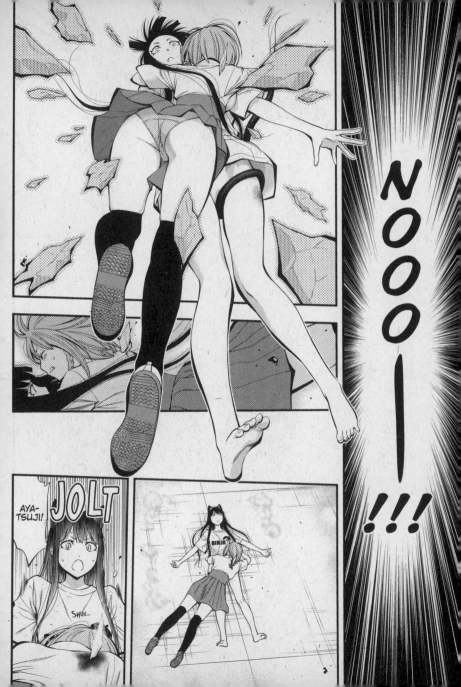

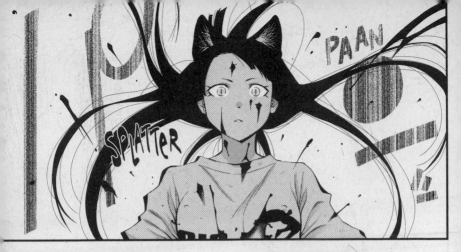

PAAN

SPLATTER

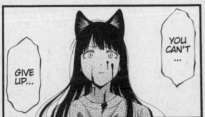

GIVE UP...

YOU CAN'T ...

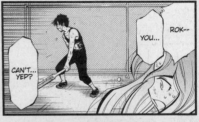

CAN'T... YEP?

YOU...

ROK--

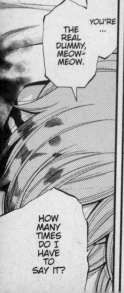

THE REAL DUMMY, MEOW-MEOW.

YOU'RE ...

HOW MANY TIMES DO I HAVE TO SAY IT?

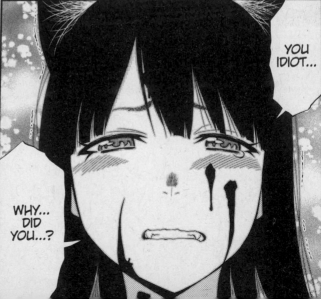

YOU IDIOT...

WHY... DID YOU...?

WE'RE...
FRIENDS, AREN'T WE?
FRIENDS...

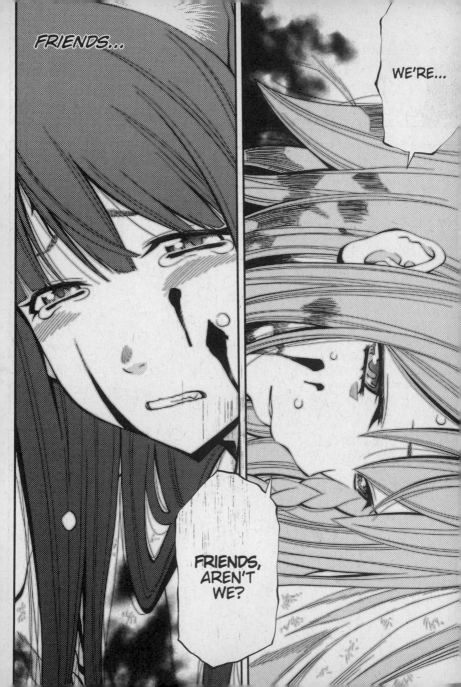

ROOO
HOW... TEDIOUS!!
OOO-
"FRIENDS"?!
WHAT?!
FRIENDSHIP AMONG YOKAI?!
OO
DON'T MAKE ME LAUGH!!
IS PRETENDING TO BE HUMAN THAT ENJOYABLE FOR YOU?!
OO
YOU YOKAI DON'T NEED FEELINGS LIKE THAT!!
YOKAI NEED TO WATCH OUT FOR THEM-SELVES ALONE!
ALL YOU HAVE TO DO IS TERROR-IZE!
OO
KILL!!
AND DEVOUR HUMANS FOR YOUR OWN SAKE!
YOUR PETTY DRAMA IS NAUSEATING TO WATCH!
SO BE IT!
I'LL SHOW YOU JUST HOW SUPERFICIAL YOUR RELATIONSHIP IS!!
CAT!!

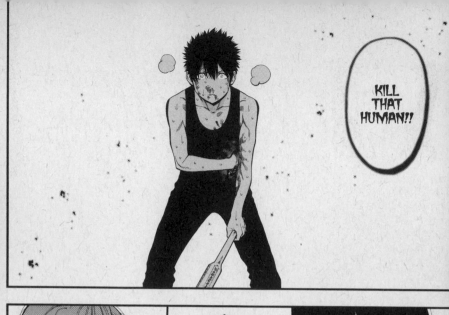

KILL THAT HUMAN!!

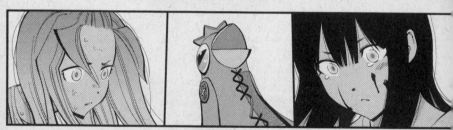

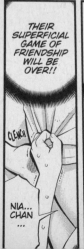

THEIR SUPERFICIAL GAME OF FRIENDSHIP WILL BE OVER!!

CLENCH

NIA... CHAN ...

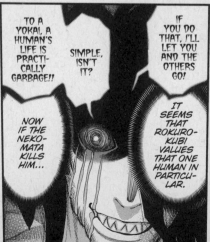

TO A YOKAI, A HUMAN'S LIFE IS PRACTI-CALLY GARBAGE!!

SIMPLE, ISN'T IT?

IF YOU DO THAT, I'LL LET YOU AND THE OTHERS GO!

NOW IF THE NEKOMATA KILLS HIM...

IT SEEMS THAT ROKURO-KUBI VALUES THAT ONE HUMAN IN PARTICU-LAR.

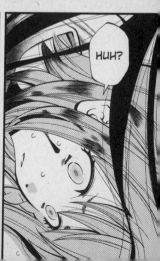

HUH?

YOU CAN'T...
OKAY ...?
I...
よろ...
NIA ... CHA ...
HEY ...
YOU WOULDN'T ...

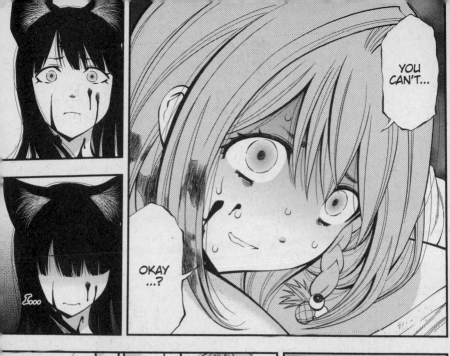

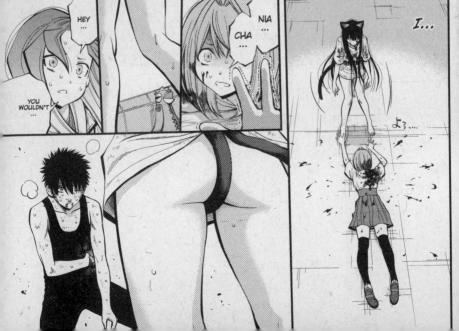

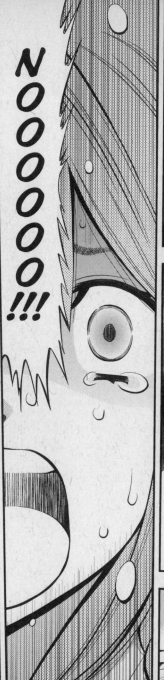

I WANT TO SAVE YOU!!

NOOOOOO!!!

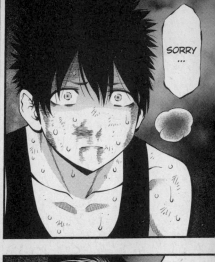

SORRY...

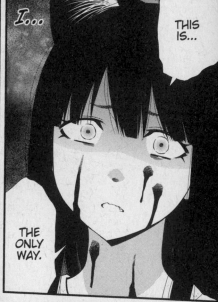

THIS IS...

Booo

THE ONLY WAY.

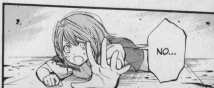

NO...

GASHU

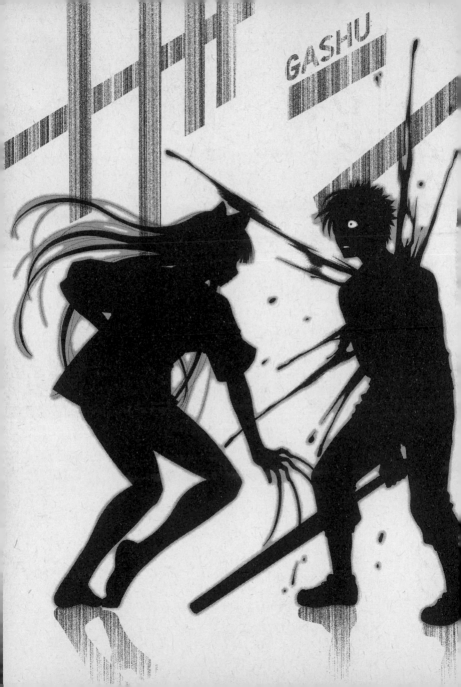

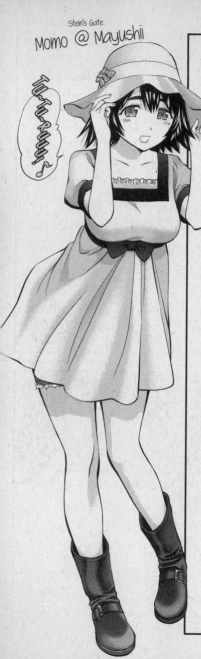

Stein's Gate
Momo @ Mayushii

Tuturuu♪

Monster Girls

Thank you very much for picking up
Yokai Girls
vol.4!

This time around, the cosplayer is Momo doing Funatsu's favorite character from *Stein's Gate*, Mayuri Shiina, a.k.a. Mayushii! ♪
But when I tried drawing her, it ended up looking like Funatsu just drew Mayushii! But well, please forgive me for that (ha ha)
Thank you very much to 5pb-sama for graciously giving me permission to draw this, as well as to Kurisu Makase on page 24!
And that cosplay was a color page! (Unfortunately, it ended up being black and white in the compiled volumes, though)
At first, I was half-joking when I talked about it with my editor. I never imagined I'd actually be able to do it! It was a lot of work to color, but also two or three or ten times more fun!
Thank you so much to all of the companies who allowed me to do this: Hara-sensei, Hashi-sensei, and Sasuga-sensei. If I have another opportunity, please let me do it again! (lol)
All righty then, so I feel like I'm doing acknowledgments in this section in every single volume, but thank you to everyone from all the shops in Akihabara who agree to cooperate with me every time, to the editorial department and all the staff and people involved in this manga. And most of all, thank you from the bottom of my heart to everyone who helped me draw this book! I'm looking forward to working with you in the future, too!

Now then, please enjoy the rest of the book. ♪

2015.3.16 Funatsu Kazuki

Official HP: http://funatsukazuki.com/
twitter @funatsukazuki
Rokka's twitter account @panyanyaruru

I tweet, too, yep!

Panyanyan!

I WANT...
GASHU
TO SAVE YOU.
37
Got to Bet on This... ♪
AH...

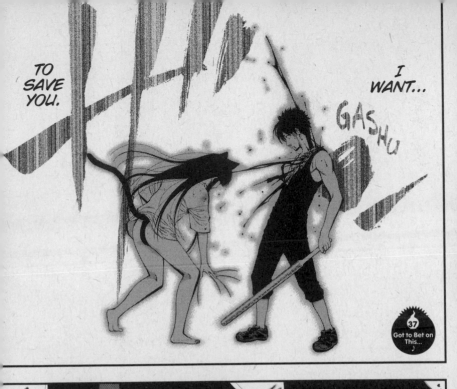

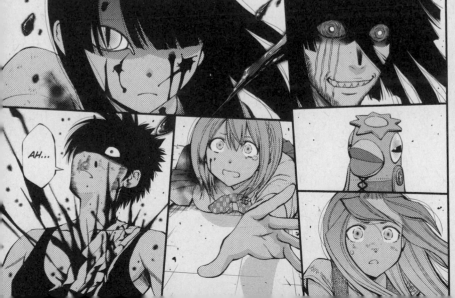

37
Got to Bet on This... ♪
NINJA
NOOOOOO!

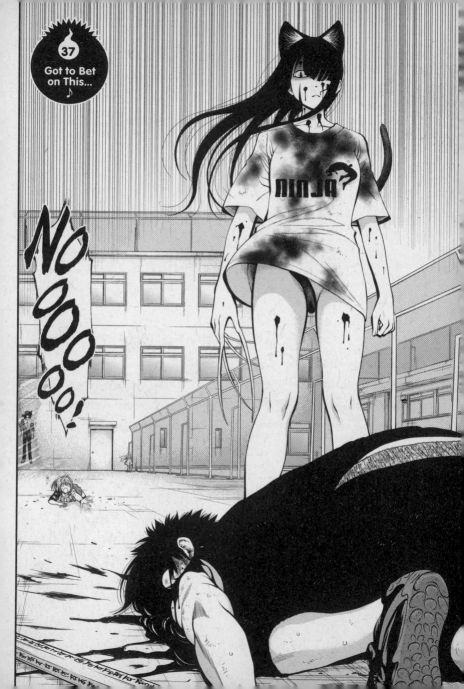

JUNKER-SAN!!
JUNKER-SAN!!
WHY, NIA-CHAN?! HOW COULD YOU?!
OH...
OH NO.
THERE'S... SO MUCH BLOOD.
I WANT--
BA-DUMP
TO LIVE?
NIA-CHAN!!
I HAD NO CHOICE ...
BUT TO BET ON THIS.
HUH?

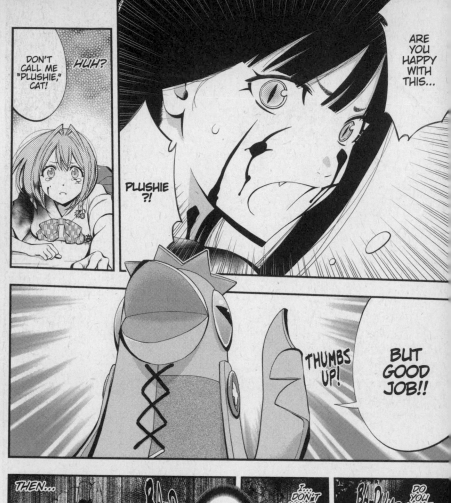

DON'T CALL ME "PLUSHIE," CAT!

HUH?

ARE YOU HAPPY WITH THIS...

PLUSHIE?!

THUMBS UP!

BUT GOOD JOB!!

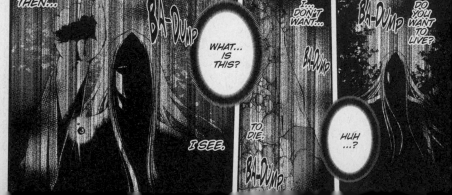

THEN...

BA-DUMP

WHAT... IS THIS?

I DON'T WANT...

BA-DUMP

DO YOU WANT TO LIVE?

I SEE.

TO DIE.

BA-DUMP

HUH...?

LIVE
BA-DUMP
KWOOOOO
WHAT?
?!
WHAT'S HAPPEN-ING?!
HIS SOUL IS...
THIS FEEL-ING...
BEING DRAWN...

I'VE SEEN THIS BEFORE!!
THAT HUMAN'S BLOOD...
OOO
FUSING WITH THE ROKURO-BOOBY'S ETHEREAL BODY!!
ROO
ふわ...
呼んでる
IT'S CALLING ME...
OO
OOO
IT'S CALLING ME...
FUWA...
OOO

KAA...
NGH ?!
GRIN

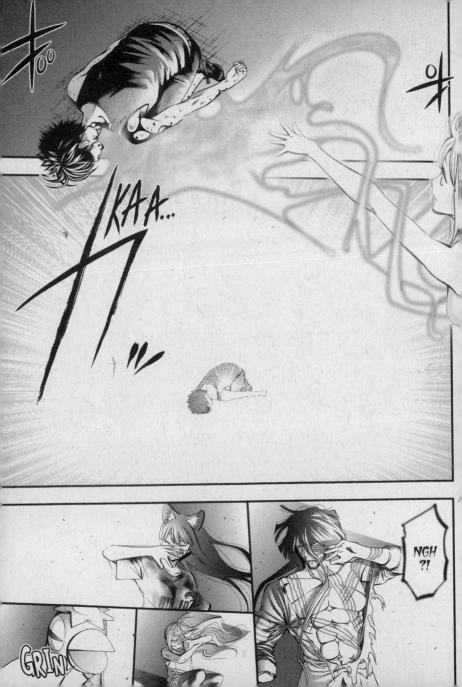

DON
Arm plate: Roku.

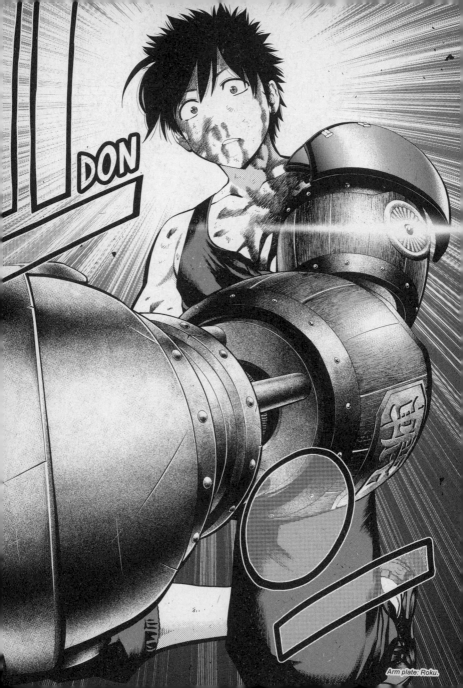

ROO
OOO
OO
WHAT ...
IS THAT?!
WH- WHOA!
IS THIS THE ETHEREAL FUSION THEY TOLD US OF?!
OOO
IT'S JUST LIKE...

ROO
A WEAPON MADE OF ETHEREAL ENERGY!!!
OO
AGAIN...
OO
OO
THIS ARM...
JUNKER-SAN!!
UNTIL NOW, WE COULDN'T GET IT TO WORK NO MATTER HOW MANY TIMES WE TRIED.
WAHHH! YOU'RE ALIVE! I THOUGHT YOU WERE DEEEAD!
I'M TOUGHER THAN I LOOK!
Though I thought I was dead, too.
BUT...
WITH THIS ARM ...!!
LET'S DO THIS!
YEP YEP!

WAUGH!!
GA-CHINK
GYURAAAAAA
GA-SHAN
HA! YOU'RE GOING TO TRY TO PUNCH ME WITH THAT ARM?!
INTRIGU-ING!!
IF YOU THINK YOU CAN BREAK MY ARMOR OF AIR...
GWO
GO AHEAD AND TRY!!
TENGU THROWING STONES... HAIL!!!
BO

HALT!!
NURI!!
DON
GAK
GAK
GAK
GAK
GAK
GAK
GAK
GAK
ICCHAN!!
I'LL BLOCK HIS ATTACKS WHILE YOU CHARGE YOUR POWER!!
DON
DON
DO
DON
JUST FOCUS ON THAT!!
DON'T UNDER-ESTIMATE ME, YOU PIDDLING ANTS!!
GWOOO
NGH...!!
DON
DON
DO
DON
DON
AAGH!!

AAAH...
KIIIIII
GIRI GIRI
GIRI
LET'S GOOOOOAAAAAGH!
GIRI
GIRI
AAAUGH...
SUPER!!
PA...
HEAVY!!!
NYA...
BOOM-STICK!!!
LET HIM HAVE IT!!!

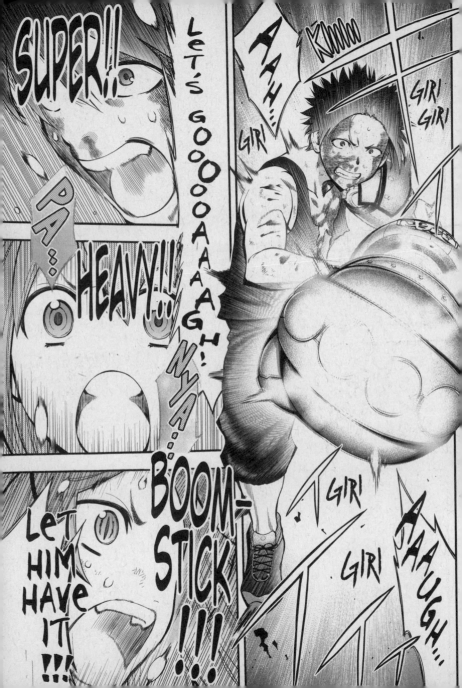

HEADBUTT BLITZ!!!!!!
NYAAAAGH!
HAAAH!!
BO
DO
DON
DON

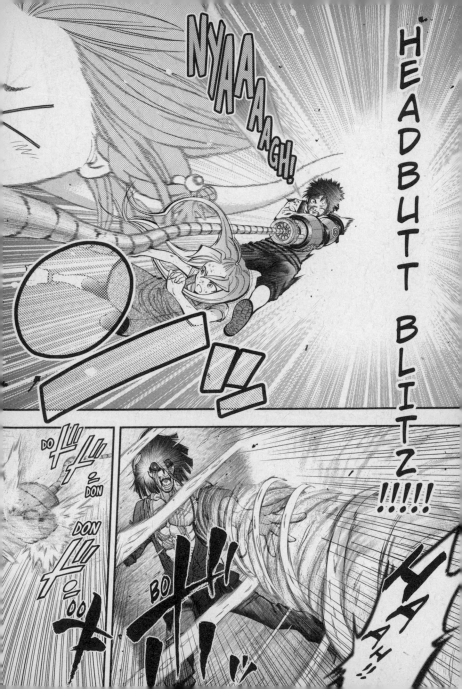

DON
DON
ROO
DON
OO

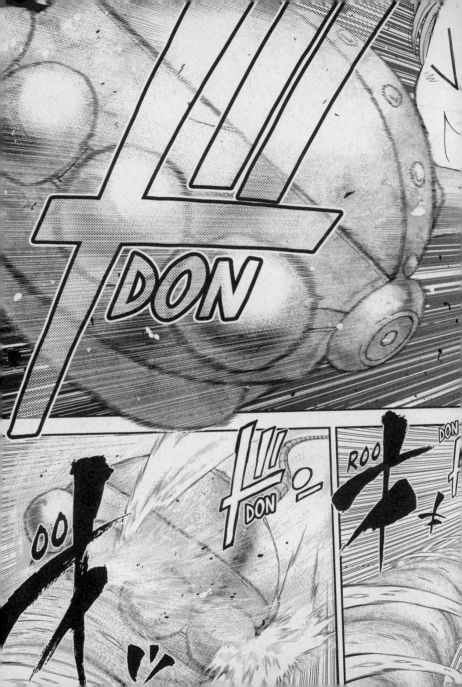

BO

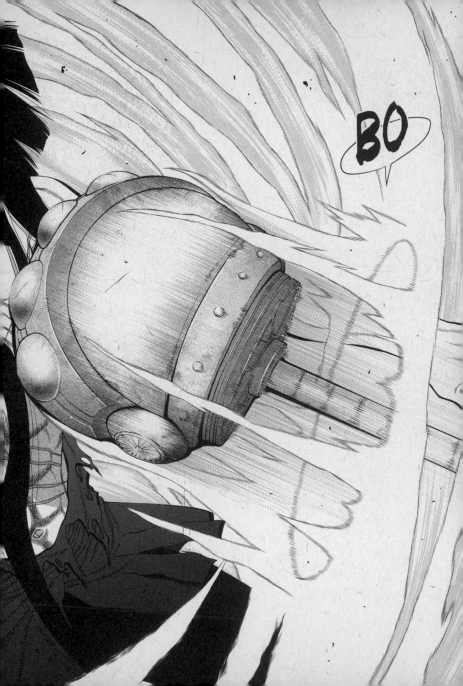

BIKI

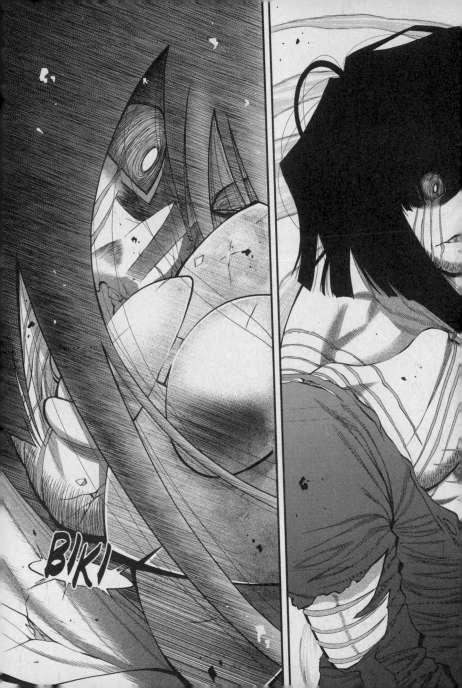

BA-GAAN

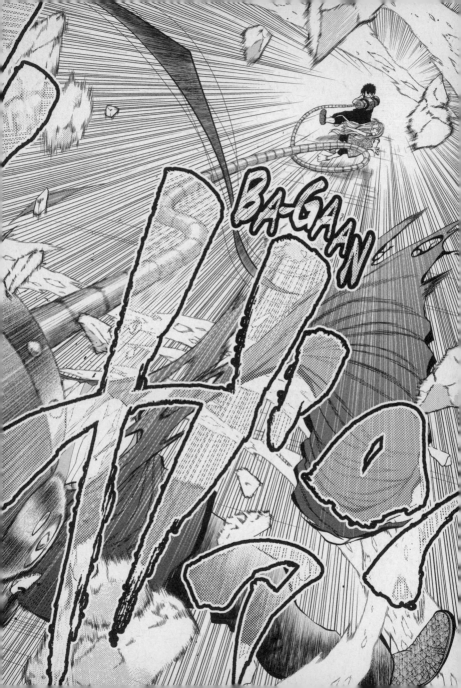

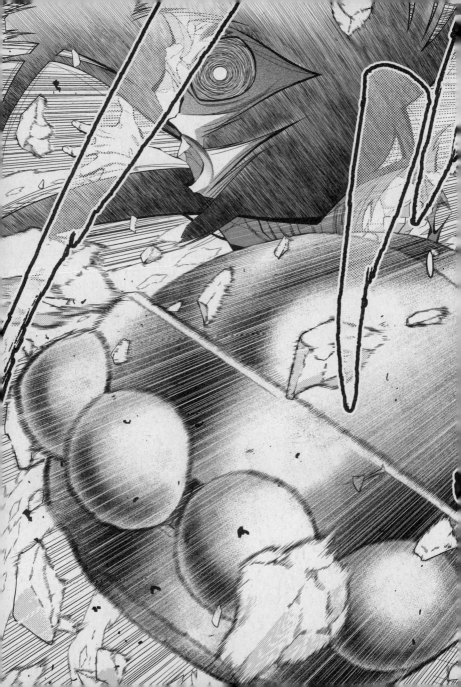

Extra: Meat Slave

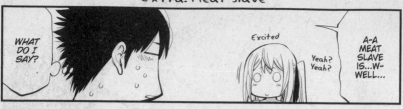

WHAT DO I SAY?

Excited

Yeah? Yeah?

A-A MEAT SLAVE IS...W-WELL...

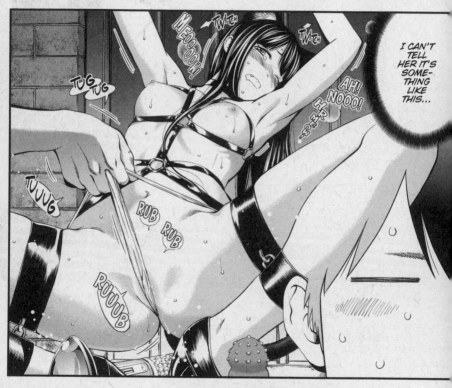

MEOOOH!

TWITCH

TWITCH

TUG TUG

AH! NOOO!

TUUUG

RUB RUB

RUUUB

I CAN'T TELL HER IT'S SOMETHING LIKE THIS...

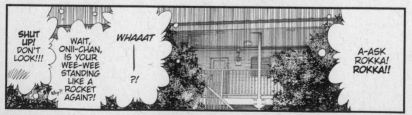

SHUT UP! DON'T LOOK!!!

WAIT, ONII-CHAN, IS YOUR WEE-WEE STANDING LIKE A ROCKET AGAIN?!

Why?!

WHAAAT ―?!

A-ASK ROKKA! ROKKA!!

38
La Puppetto
Pri...pu...pe...
♪
THUMBS UP

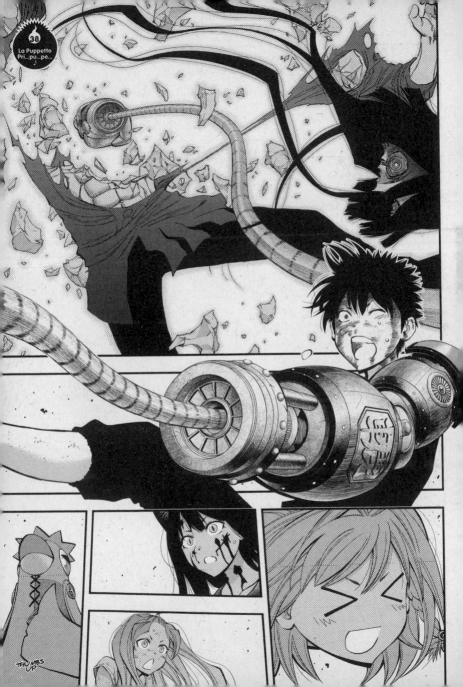

38
La Puppetto
Pri...pu...pe...
♪
OOO
OO

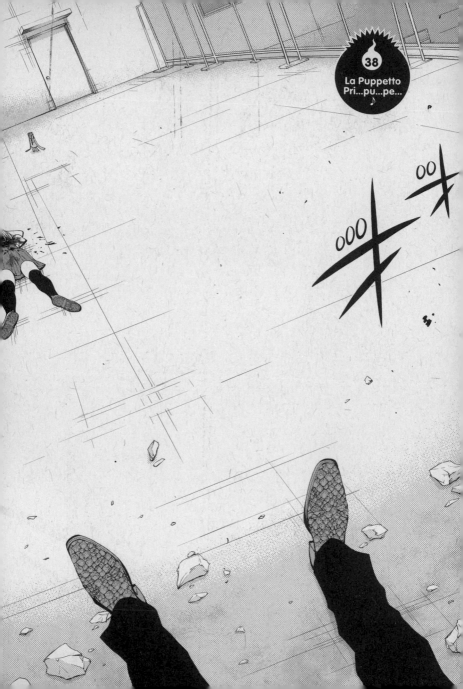

OO
GA-CHINK
OOO
HAAAH!
HAAAH... HAAAH...
OO
OO
DID WE...
WIN?
OO
HEH!
WHAT DESTRUC- TIVE POWER ...!
THE SORAGAMI WAS SHATTERED TO PIECES.
HM?
PIECES ?!
What?

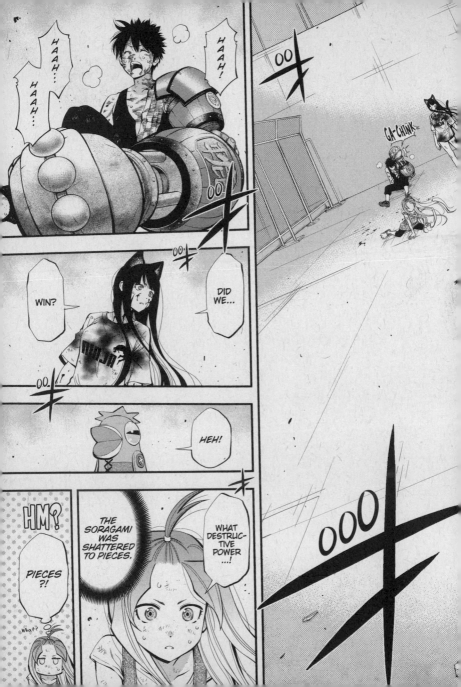

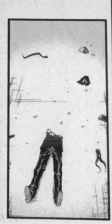

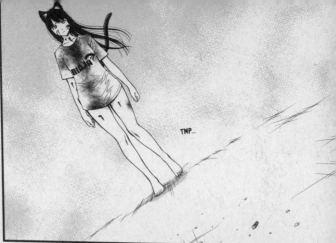

TMP...

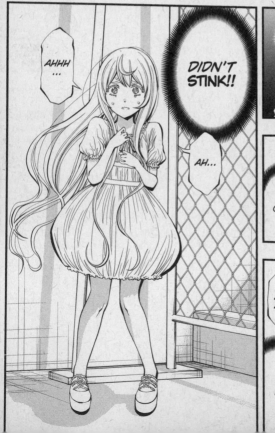

AHHH
...

DIDN'T
STINK!!

AH...

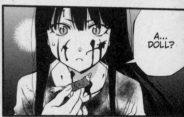

A...
DOLL?

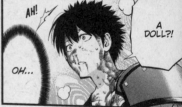

AH!

OH...

A
DOLL?!

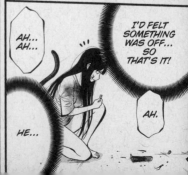

I'D FELT
SOMETHING
WAS OFF...
SO
THAT'S IT!

AH...
AH...

AH.

HE...

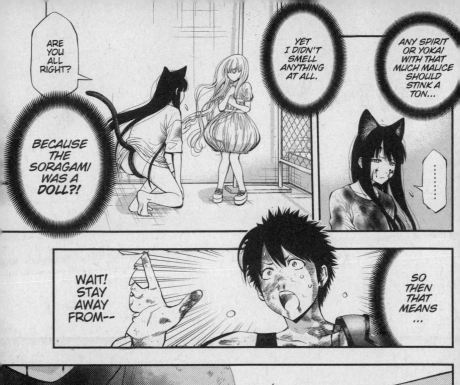

ARE YOU ALL RIGHT?

YET I DIDN'T SMELL ANYTHING AT ALL.

ANY SPIRIT OR YOKAI WITH THAT MUCH MALICE SHOULD STINK A TON...

BECAUSE THE SORAGAMI WAS A DOLL?!

......

WAIT! STAY AWAY FROM--

SO THEN THAT MEANS...

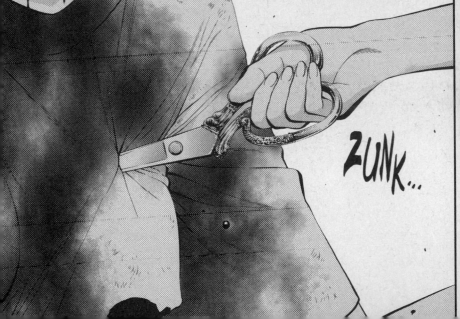

ZUNK...

AH...!
GUWA
HOW FUCKING DARE YOU?!
YOU DIRTY, STINKING CAAAAAT!!!

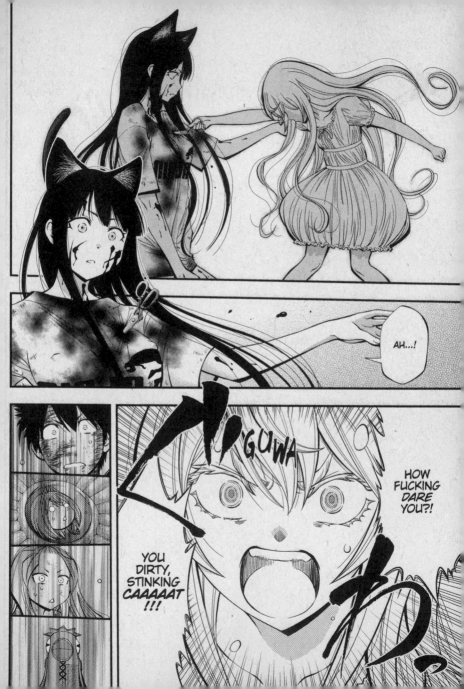

IF YOU ONLY KNEW HOW MUCH TIME AND EFFORT I POURED INTO MAKING THAT TEN-CHAN DOLL!
KICK
THREE YEARS! THREE YEARS, I TELL YOU!!
WHACK
THWACK
YOU THINK I'VE GOT TIME TO WASTE, LIKE YOU STUPID FUCKING YOKAI? YOU MEAT-FOR-BRAINS!!
URK!
HER ATTACKS ARE PURELY PHYSI-CAL!!
ZUN
NO WAY... YOU'RE...
THAT GIRL IS...
HUMAN ?!
THAT'S RIGHT. I'M A GODDAMN HUMAN!
DON'T THINK I'M ANYTHING LIKE YOU FUCKWADS!
MY NAME'S FIORE!
FIORE THE PUPPET-MASTER!
THEY CALL ME LA PUPPETTO PRINCIPESSA!

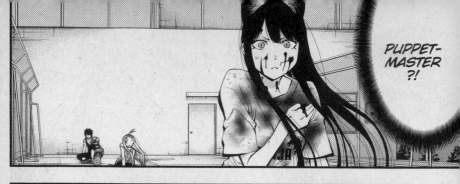

PUPPET-MASTER?!

SO THAT TENGU WAS...A PUPPET?!

AND THIS CHILD WAS THE ONE CONTROLLING IT?!

IS SHE...

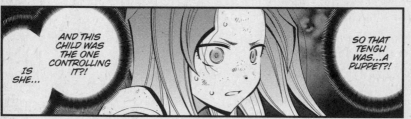

A MONSTER?!

RUSTLE RUSTLE

PLIP PLIP...

BITE

YOU'RE DYING ANYWAY, SO THESE GUYS'LL BE ENOUGH...

ZU ZU ZU

ZU

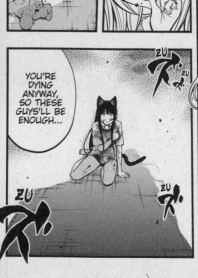

TUNK

TUNK

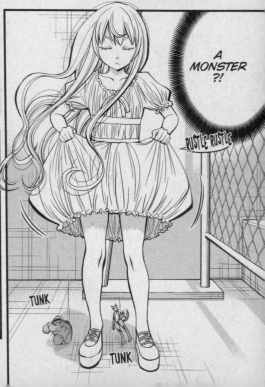

ZU
TO FINISH YOU OFF!
ZU
ZU
SHII: TALES OF THIS YOKAI ARE TOLD IN WAKAYAMA, HIROSHIMA, AND YAMAGUCHI. SAID TO KILL AND EAT CATTLE, IT'S SMART AND FAST.
AKA-ATAMA: THIS SUPER-HUMANLY STRONG MAN WAS SAID TO HAVE ACTUALLY LIVED IN TOTTORI. HE WAS APPARENTLY STRONG ENOUGH TO BE ABLE TO CARRY A LADDER WEIGHTED WITH TWELVE BAGS OF RICE.
ZU
LET'S DO THIS! ORAA!
DO
DO DO
DO
!

SHUUU
TSK... I USED UP TOO MUCH SPIRITUAL POWER ON TEN-CHAN!
I GUESS I CAN'T DO TWO!
ORAA!!
DOON
GAGH!
DO
DO
DO
DO
DO
DO
ORA ORA ORA ORA ORA ORA ORA ORA ORA ORA ORA ORA ORA ORA ORA ORA ORA!
DO
DO
GRAB
YANK
!!

ORA ORA ORA ORA ORA ORA ORA ORA ORA ORA!
BA-TAN
BA-TAN
BA-TA AN
BA-TAN
ORA ORA ORA ORA ORA ORA!
GAK...
URH...
AHA HA HA HA HA HA HA!
DRIP...
DIE DIE DIE DIE DIE DIE DIE DIE!!
NGH... ARE HER SPIRITUAL POWERS BOTTOMLESS?!
SHE HAS EVEN MORE THAN THE LAD!
ROKKA! CAN YOU FIRE OFF ONE MORE SHOT?!
H-HOLD ON A SEC...

DANGLE
GUH... UGH...
HEH HEH! ♪ NOT SO PRISSY NOW EH, KITTY-CAT?
THIS IS YOUR LAST CHANCE, 'KAY?
BE MY PET!
IF I HAD YOU AS A PET, NOW *THAT* WOULD BE SOMETHING TO BRAG ABOUT!
YEAH!
I'LL CALL YOU NERO! *NERO AFORTUNADO!*
LICK
IT MEANS "LUCKY BLACK," YOU KNOW?
SO? NICE, HUH?
......

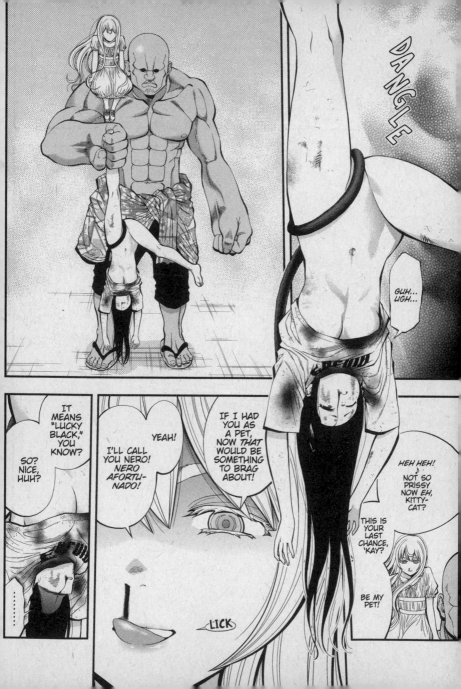

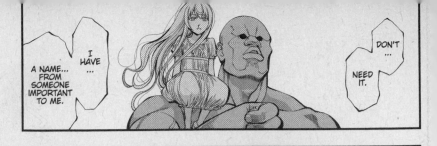

A NAME... FROM SOMEONE IMPORTANT TO ME.

I HAVE ...

DON'T ...

NEED IT.

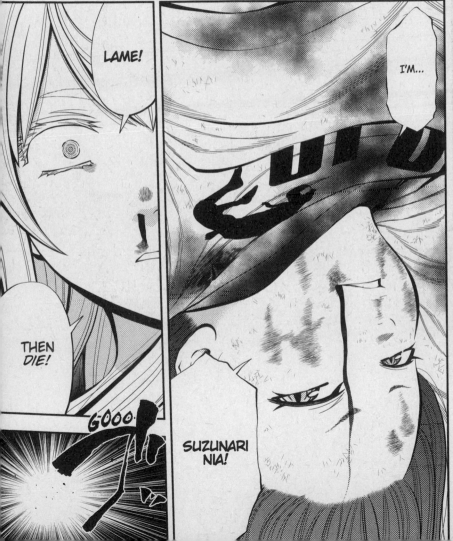

LAME!

I'M...

THEN *DIE!*

GOOO...

SUZUNARI NIA!

KAPPA THE RIPPER!!!
BA-BAAN
SLICE...!!
HEH!
SPARKLE
BEEN A WHILE SINCE I GOT TO DO THAT!

WHAAA?!!
HEY...
NOOOO!!!
DARK CAT SCRATCH, FIRST BLADE...
WHIRLWIND SLICE!
旋
斬

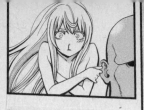

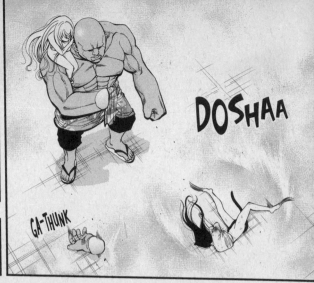

DOSHAA

SMIRK

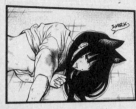

GA-THUNK

YOU...

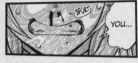

SPURTS

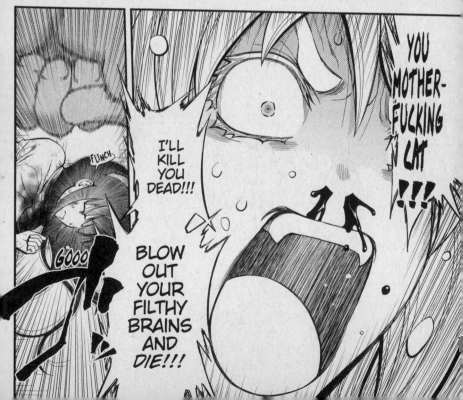

FLINCH

GOOO

I'LL KILL YOU DEAD!!!

BLOW OUT YOUR FILTHY BRAINS AND DIE!!!

YOU MOTHER-FUCKING CAT!!!

DON!!

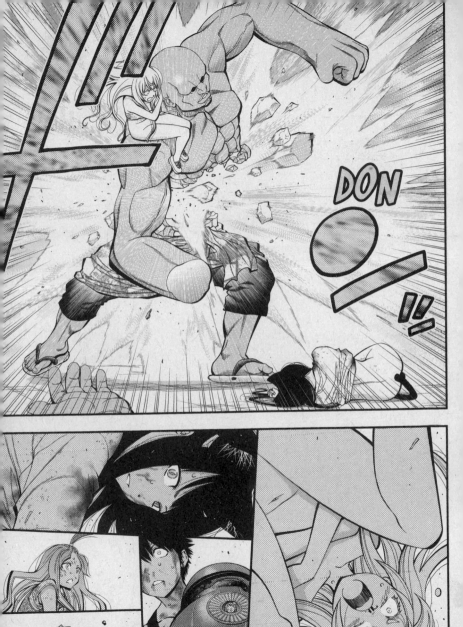

CUT IT OUT!

YOU'VE LOST THIS ONE...
HANAKO!
DON

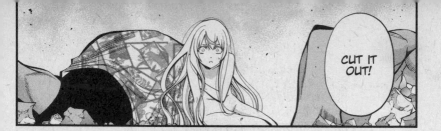

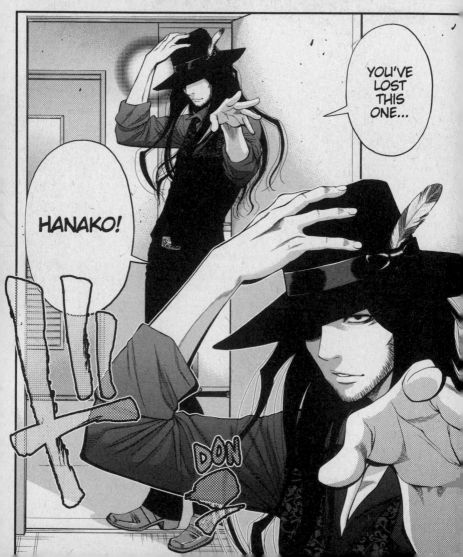

39
The Wind Stopped...
YOU'VE LOST THIS ONE...
HANAKO!
TAP

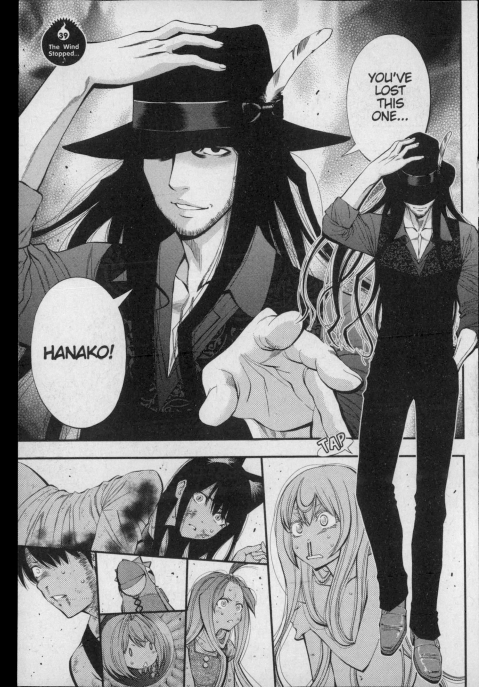

PANIC PANIC
T-T-TEN-CHAN?!
PANIC
TUMP
TUMP
WH-WHY ARE YOU HE--
BOFF
BWA!
SHUT UP!
ZU
I THOUGHT I TOLD YOU...
DON'T MAKE A PUPPET BASED ON ME.
ZU
ZU
ZU
AH!
WELL ...
PANIC PANIC
TREMBLE TREMBLE TREMBLE
THIS IS...
UM, UH...
PANIC PANIC
TREMBLE TREMBLE TREMBLE

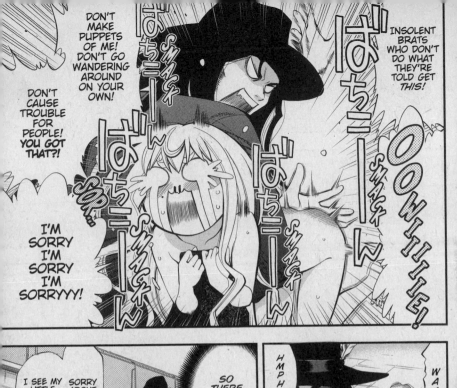

DON'T MAKE PUPPETS OF ME! DON'T GO WANDERING AROUND ON YOUR OWN!

DON'T CAUSE TROUBLE FOR PEOPLE! YOU GOT THAT?!

INSOLENT BRATS WHO DON'T DO WHAT THEY'RE TOLD GET THIS!

I'M SORRY I'M SORRY I'M SORRYYY!

OOWIIIE!

I SEE MY LITTLE IDIOT HAS BEEN CAUSING TROUBLE FOR YOU.

Can you stand?

SORRY ABOUT THAT.

SO THERE IS A REAL SORA-GAMI!

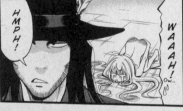

HMPH!

WAAAH!

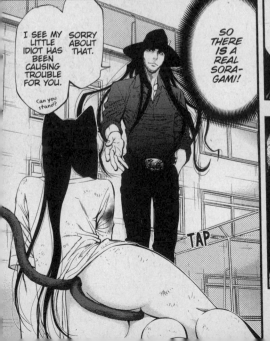

TAP

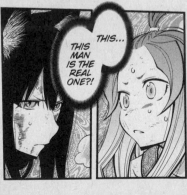

THIS... THIS MAN IS THE REAL ONE?!

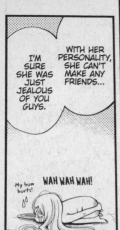

I'M SURE SHE WAS JUST JEALOUS OF YOU GUYS.

WITH HER PERSONALITY, SHE CAN'T MAKE ANY FRIENDS...

WAH WAH WAH!

My bum hurts!

BUT SHE'S SUCH A BRAT, I DON'T KNOW WHAT TO DO WITH HER.

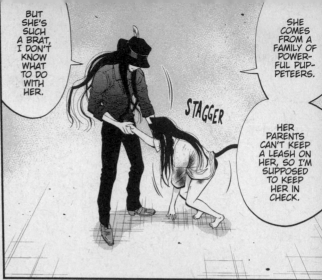

STAGGER

SHE COMES FROM A FAMILY OF POWERFUL PUPPETEERS.

HER PARENTS CAN'T KEEP A LEASH ON HER, SO I'M SUPPOSED TO KEEP HER IN CHECK.

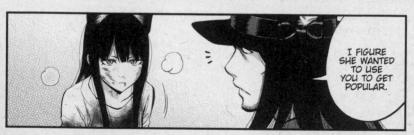

I FIGURE SHE WANTED TO USE YOU TO GET POPULAR.

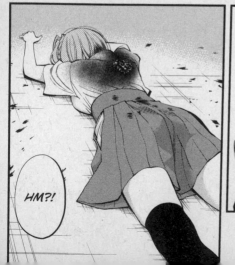

HM?!

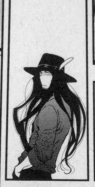

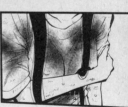

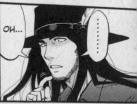

OH...

THAT'S MORE LIKE IT!
SMOOSH SMOOSH
TWIDDLE TWIDDLE TWIDDLE TWIDDLE
...
GYAAAAAAAH!!!
HANDS OFF, BUSTER!!!
WHOA... HEY!!
DON

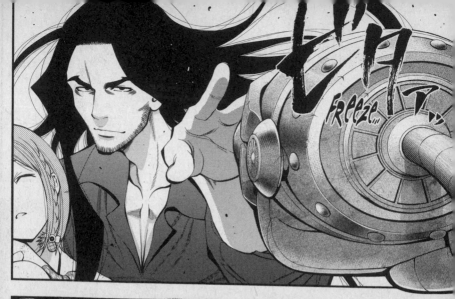

FREEZE...

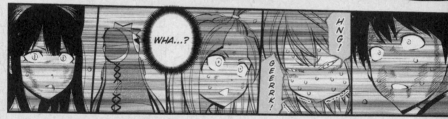

WHA...?

HNG!

GEERRK!

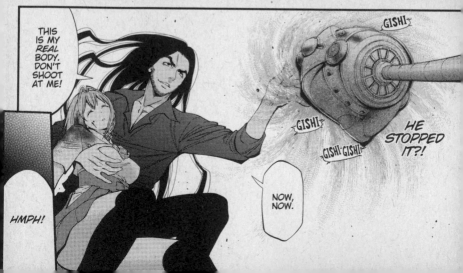

THIS IS MY *REAL* BODY. DON'T SHOOT AT ME!

GISHI

GISHI

GISHI GISHI

HE STOPPED IT?!

NOW, NOW.

HMPH!

THE BLOOD OF THE GUARD-IAN...
SURE IS CAPRI-CIOUS.
HUH? WHAT?
IT SEEMS LIKE YOU'LL BE A PROBLEM DOWN THE LINE...
ZU
ZU
I THINK...
ZU
IT'S BETTER FOR YOU TO DIE HERE AND SAVE MY-SELF THE TROUBLE.
ZU
!!
ZU
WHA ...?
WHOA!
ZU
ZU
......
ZU

OO
OO
ROO
OO

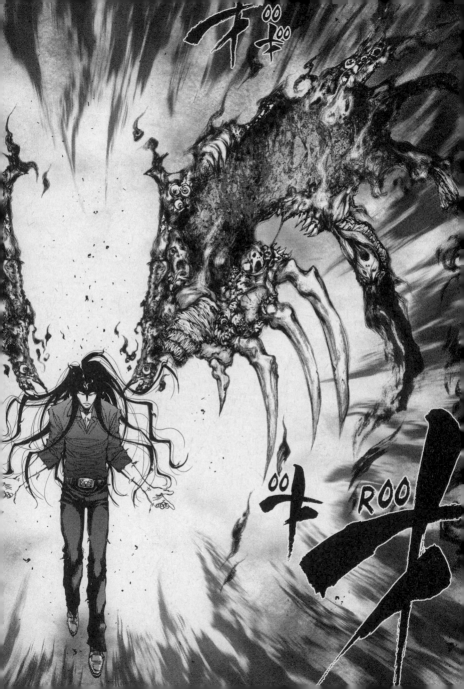

NGH!
OH...
HE STINKS!
I CAN HARDLY BREATHE!
AH
AGH!
AH!
HIS POWERFUL YOKAI ENERGY IS SUCKING LESSER YOKAI TOWARDS HIM.
AGH!
BUCHU
BUCHU
BICHUN

GWO
GWO
GWO
GWO
GWO

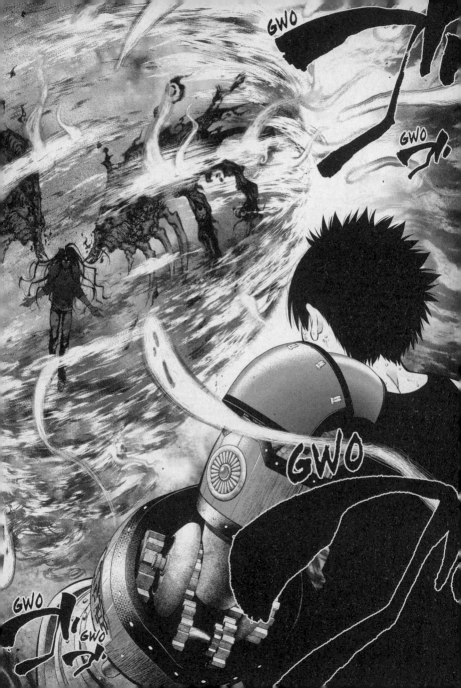

WHAT THE HELL... IS THIS?
GWO
AH...
IT'S NO USE...
ROO
GWO
AHH...
IT'S SUCKING UP OUR FEAR.
OO
AH...
I'M WEAKEN-ING.
KIIN

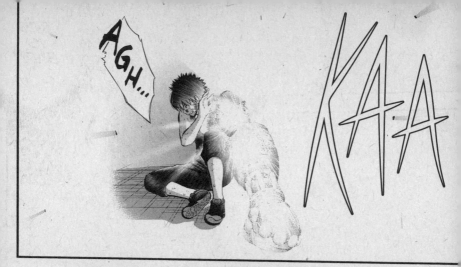

AGH...

KA·A

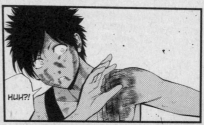

AH!

HUH?!

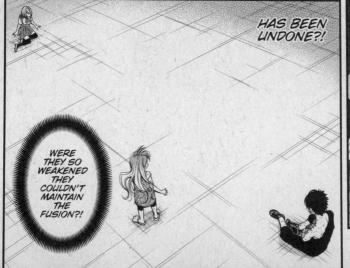

HAS BEEN UNDONE?!

WERE THEY SO WEAKENED THEY COULDN'T MAINTAIN THE FUSION?!

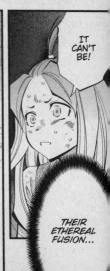

IT CAN'T BE!

THEIR ETHEREAL FUSION...

THIS IS BAD!!
ROO
WE CAN'T FIGHT THIS MAN!!
HE'S NOT AN OPPONENT WE COULD BEAT, NO MATTER HOW HARD WE--
SUU
OO
PAKYU...
OO
GOOO

AHHH!
BWOO
......
?!
EEK!
WOO
DO
DO DO
......
!!
NGH!
EUGH!
WHAT?! A GUST FROM BEHIND ...
!
THAT'S... NO WAY!

PLASMA?!!
KWOOOO
HE INSTANTLY COMPRESSED AIR...
AND USED THE IMMENSE THERMAL ENERGY IT EMITTED TO BREAK AWAY ELECTRONS FROM THE MOLECULES THAT COMPRISE THE GAS...
TO MAKE PLASMA!!
THE HEAT OF PLASMA IS BETWEEN A THOUSAND AND A HUNDRED MILLION DEGREES!!
AHH...
IF WE'RE HIT BY THAT, IT DOESN'T MATTER IF WE'RE HUMAN OR YOKAI...
WE'D ALL BE OBLITERATED!!
AH!
DIE!

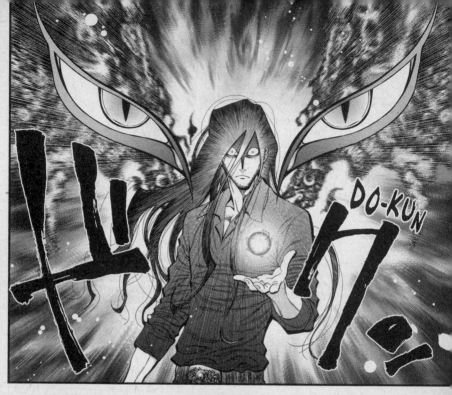

DO-KUN

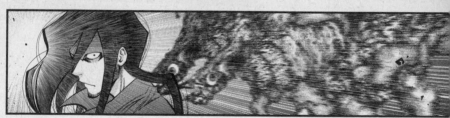

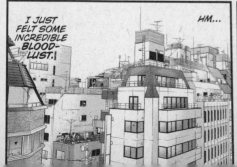

I JUST FELT SOME INCREDIBLE BLOOD-LUST.

HM...

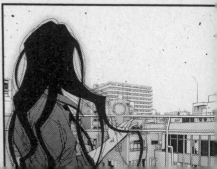

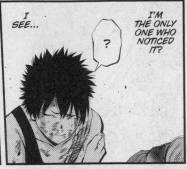

AND THE ONLY ONE WITH THE SKILLS TO DO THAT WOULD BE...

SOMEONE SHOT THEIR YOKAI POWER TOWARD ME ONLY.

HMPH!

I SEE...

?

I'M THE ONLY ONE WHO NOTICED IT?

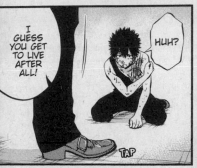

I GUESS YOU GET TO LIVE AFTER ALL!

HUH?

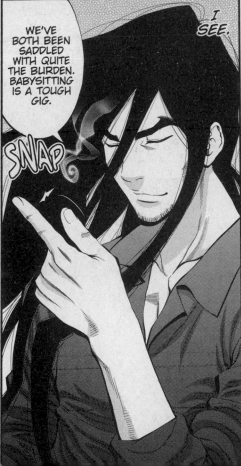

WE'VE BOTH BEEN SADDLED WITH QUITE THE BURDEN. BABYSITTING IS A TOUGH GIG.

I SEE.

SNAP

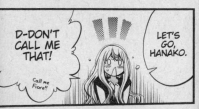

D-DON'T CALL ME THAT!

Call me Fiore!!

LET'S GO, HANAKO.

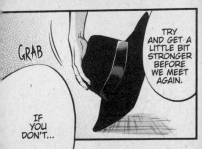

GRAB

TRY AND GET A LITTLE BIT STRONGER BEFORE WE MEET AGAIN.

IF YOU DON'T...

I'LL KILL YOU WITHOUT EVEN BREAKING A SWEAT.
AND DON'T YOU DARE FORGET THAT...
BEARER OF THE BLOOD OF THE GUARDIAN!
TEN-CHAN! CARRY ME ON YOUR SHOULDERS! ♡
DOES THAT MEAN I CAN CUT OFF YOUR SHORT LITTLE LEGS?
THEY'RE NOT SHORT!!
SLAM
BA...
BLEAH!

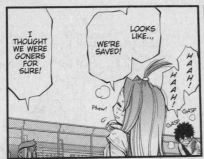

I THOUGHT WE WERE GONERS FOR SURE!

WE'RE SAVED!

LOOKS LIKE...

HAAH! HAAH! HAAH!

GASP

Phew!

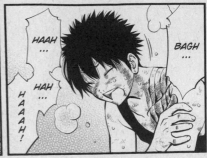

HAAH...

HAH...

HAAAH...

BAGH...

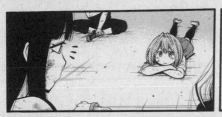

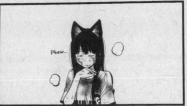

Phew...

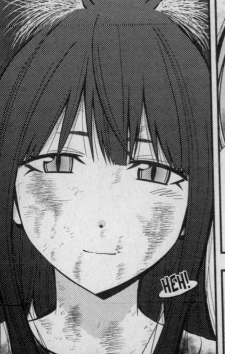

HEH!

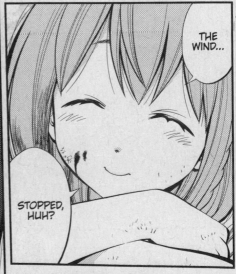

THE WIND...

STOPPED, HUH?

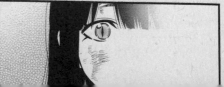

YEAH!

Yokai Girls ❹ End

Yokai Field Guide!

Introducing the yokai Yatsuki encounters, *Yokai Girls*-style!

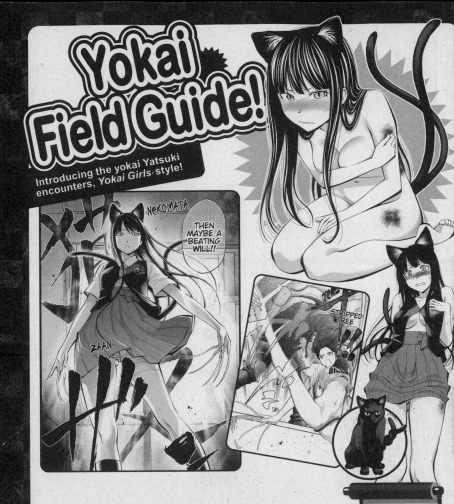

NEKOMATA

THEN MAYBE A BEATING WILL!!

ZAAN

STRIPPED TREE

Stories of this cat yokai figure in folk legends and classic ghost stories all over Japan. The first appearance of a nekomata is said to be recorded in *Meigetsuki,* from the early Kamakura period, in which a monster named a nekomata devours seven or eight people in one night. In Yamanaka, records of nekomata report creatures of larger sizes, as big as lions or leopards. There are also anecdotes of the nekomata which led to the naming of certain mountains, such as Nekomata-yama in Fujiyama and Nekomaga-oka in Fukushima.

First Appearance: Chapter 30

猫又

NEKOMATA

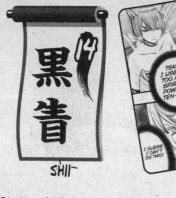

黒眚

14

SHII

Stories of this yokai are told of in western Japan. It is a beast that preys on cows. In Wakayama and Hiroshima, they say that you can prod cows along by calling out *shii, shii*, as it means, "There's a Shii behind you."

First Appearance: Chapter 38

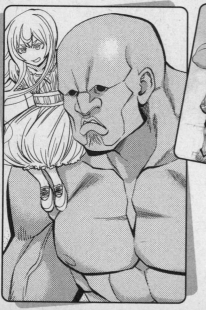

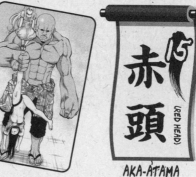

赤頭

15

(RED HEAD)

AKA-ATAMA

A mysterious and super-humanly strong man called "Aka-atama" was said to have actually lived in Tottori prefecture. They say that after his death, young people of his village would spend the night by his grave in order to be-stowed with his strength.

First Appearance: Chapter 38

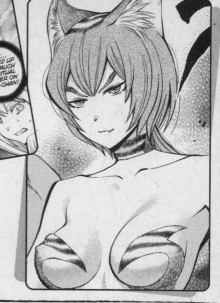

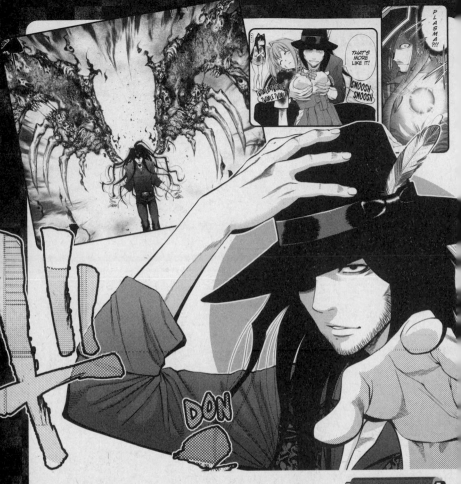

In Nara prefecture, tengu are called soragami. The various legends about tengu show how the Japanese people revere mountains. In Yamagata, mossy or sandy areas between thickets in the mountains are called "tengu's sumo rings." While in Kanagawa, the sound of a large tree being cut down is referred to as "a tengu-felling." The popular image of tengu is the red-faced sort with long noses, or bird tengu, but in folk tradition they're often described as more ethereal in nature, or as creatures that don't show themselves.

First Appearance: Chapter 38

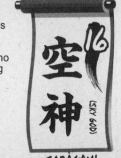

To be continued!

YATSUKI-KUN'S PAY.
Uh-huh.
NYAAAAAAH!
Akihabara UDX
Yodobashi Camera Yuurindou
JR Akihabara Station
Fureai Bridge
TUP TUP
ROKKA?
302
Soup Curry Kamui

YŌKAI GIRLS
AKIBA MAP
N
W
E
S
Sankou Rare Item Shop
Maid Cafe Pinafore Third Branch
Don Quijote
Tora no Ana Flagship Akihabara Shops
437
Belle Salle Akihabara
sofmap
Kanda Myoujinshita
Comic Zin
Soto-Kanda 2 Chome
Akihabara Dai Building
Melon Books
SEGA
17
GAMERS
Radio Kaikan
K-Books

SEVEN SEAS' GHOST SHIP PRESENTS

YOKAI GIRLS

story and art by KAZUKI FUNATSU

VOL.4

TRANSLATION
Jennifer Ward

ADAPTATION
Bambi Eloriaga-Amago

LETTERING AND LAYOUT
Phil Christie

COVER DESIGN
Nicky Lim

PROOFREADER
Janet Houck
Stephanie Cohen

EDITOR
Shannon Fay

PRODUCTION ASSISTANT
CK Russell

PRODUCTION MANAGER
Lissa Pattillo

EDITOR-IN-CHIEF
Adam Arnold

PUBLISHER
Jason DeAngelis

ISBN: 978-1-947804-13-5

Printed in Canada

First Printing: September 2018

10 9 8 7 6 5 4 3 2 1

FOLLOW US ONLINE: *www.ghostshipmanga.com*

READING DIRECTIONS

This book reads from *right to left*, Japanese style.
If this is your first time reading manga, you start
reading from the top right panel on each page and
take it from there. If you get lost, just follow the
numbered diagram here. It may seem backwards at
first, but you'll get the hang of it! Have fun!!

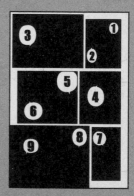